BEAUTIFUL BRUTALITY

How to use Branding to Convert Strangers into Raving Fans

TERRY SHAND

Disclaimer

There are always exceptions to the rules laid out in this book. Rather than mentioning it multiple times throughout the book, I'm stating it once upfront so we can dive into the good stuff.

Here are a few examples of 'vanilla' brands that have done well for themselves. The exceptions to the rules, or as I like to call them, 'The Beige Unicorns':

The Beige Unicorns

Sure, most beige brands get buried in the marketing graveyard. But every now and then, a few manage to stumble into success without ever growing a spine.

Coca-Cola: The beige soda that became the global IV drip of sugar. Their "brand personality" is literally bubbles and a Santa Claus they rented out from folklore. Yet they're so entrenched in culture that they could release *Diet Beige* tomorrow, and people would still guzzle it.

Visa: A brand so aggressively vanilla its tagline might as well be "We Exist." Yet they own the financial bloodstream of the planet. You don't feel passion for Visa. You feel nothing. Which is exactly their superpower. Nobody ever got fired for swiping it.

Colgate: A toothpaste so bland its packaging looks like hospital signage. But when's the last time you saw a Colgate ad that made you feel anything? Exactly. And yet they're brushing down billions. Sometimes being the boring default is enough.

Band-Aid: They've sung the same lullaby since 1920: "I'm stuck on Band-Aid, cause Band-Aid's stuck on me." No edge, no controversy, just sterile beige comfort. And somehow they became the Kleenex of wounds.

McDonald's (to a point): Yes, they've flirted with edgier campaigns, but let's be honest: "I'm Lovin' It" is basically marketing oatmeal. It's not brutal, it's not brave. But damn if it doesn't print money every second of every day.

In this book, we're going to discuss the opposite of those 'Beige Unicorns': brands that break rules and thrive because of it.

Let's dive in.

Contents

INTRODUCTION
Your Brand Is Already Dead

You just don't know it yet.

Right now, somewhere in a conference room that smells like stale coffee and broken dreams, a marketing team is crafting another forgettable campaign. They're debating whether "innovative solutions" sounds better than "cutting-edge technology." They're A/B testing their way to beige. They're focus-grouping the soul out of what could have been something magnificent.

Meanwhile, their brand is flatlining.

Not dramatically; that would at least be interesting. No, it's dying the corporate equivalent of death by a thousand paper cuts: ignored social posts, skipped ads, and the soul-crushing sound of customers saying "Who?" when your company name comes up at dinner parties.

Welcome to the graveyard of nice brands. Population: everyone trying to play it safe.

The Conspiracy of Comfortable

Here's what they don't teach you in business school: the entire marketing industrial complex is designed to make you fail politely. Every "best practice" is optimized for mediocrity. Every template is pre-approved for blandness. Every consultant who promises to "elevate your brand voice" is actually teaching you to whisper in a hurricane.

They've convinced you that offense is the enemy. That polarization is poison. That the goal is universal appeal, as if being everyone's second choice is somehow better than being someone's first obsession.

It's a lie. A comfortable, profitable lie that keeps agencies and CMOs employed and everyone safely, quietly, predictably unsuccessful.

The truth? The brands you remember, the ones that changed your behavior, earned your loyalty, or made you feel something real, all broke the rules. Every single one. They chose beautiful brutality over beautiful bullshit.

Why This Book Will Piss People Off

Fair warning: this book is not written for the faint of heart or the politically correct. It's not for brands that want to be liked. It's for brands that want to be remembered, revered, and resurrected in the stories people tell about the companies that mattered.

If you picked up this book hoping for gentle guidance on "finding your authentic voice," put it down. Go buy something with a pastel cover and a subtitle about "mindful marketing." This isn't that book.

This is for the rebels who are tired of being ignored. The founders who know their product deserves more than polite applause. The marketers who are sick of campaigns that perform like sedatives: technically working, but putting everyone to sleep.

This book will teach you to weaponize honesty, polarize with purpose, and turn your brand into the kind of force that stops people mid-scroll and makes them choose sides. Some will love you. Others will hate you. Everyone will remember you.

And that's exactly the point.

The Beautiful Brutality Manifesto

Let's get one thing straight: brutal doesn't mean cruel. It doesn't mean attacking people or communities or vulnerabilities. Beautiful brutality is something far more sophisticated and far more dangerous to mediocrity.

Beautiful brutality is:

- **Honesty without apology**: saying what everyone thinks but no one dares voice

- **Clarity without compromise**: knowing exactly who you serve and who you're willing to lose
- **Conviction without cowardice**: standing for something even when it's uncomfortable
- **Style without safety**: making bold choices that make people feel something

It's the difference between Nike saying "Just Do It" and some forgettable athletic brand saying "Achieve Your Goals with Our Performance Gear." One stops you cold. The other slides past like elevator music.

Beautiful brutality built empires while nice brands planned their own funerals.

What You'll Learn (And Unlearn)

This book is structured like a deprogramming course. Each chapter will systematically destroy one sacred cow of conventional marketing wisdom and replace it with something that actually works.

You'll learn why "offending no one" is the fastest way to excite no one. Why polarization isn't the enemy of good business; it's the engine. Why the brands that trigger the strongest reactions often end up with the most devoted followers.

You'll discover the neuroscience behind why our brains are wired to pay attention to controversy and ignore comfort.

You'll see case studies of brands that bet everything on brutal honesty and won. You'll also see the smoking wreckage of companies that played it safe until they played themselves out of existence.

But most importantly, you'll learn how to diagnose your own brand's terminal case of niceness and prescribe the brutal medicine that will bring it back to life.

Your Comfortable Lies Are Showing

Before we go any further, let's address the voice in your head that's already making excuses:

"But our industry is different." No, it's not. Every industry has brands that break through and brands that blend in. The difference isn't the sector; it's the spine.

"But we can't afford to alienate potential customers." You can't afford not to. In a world where attention is the scarcest resource, being forgettable is financial suicide.

"But what if we offend someone?" Here's a harder question: what if no one notices you exist?

The biggest risk isn't controversy. It's invisibility. And invisibility is guaranteed when you try to be everything to everyone.

The Death of Vanilla

Here's what vanilla brands don't understand: neutrality is not neutral. When you choose to stand for nothing, you're making a statement. You're saying you're too weak to have an opinion. Too scared to take a side. Too afraid of conflict to fight for anything that matters.

Customers see that weakness. They sense the fear. And they respond by giving their attention, loyalty, and money to brands with enough backbone to stand for something, even if that something isn't universally loved.

The vanilla brands think they're playing it safe. In reality, they're choosing the most dangerous strategy of all: being forgettable in an age where memory equals market share.

Your Uncomfortable Assignment

As you read this book, you'll be forced to confront some uncomfortable questions about your brand:

- What are you so afraid of saying that it might be exactly what you need to say?
- Who are you trying so hard not to offend that you've forgotten who you're trying to serve?
- What truth about your industry is everyone whispering but no one shouting?
- If your brand had to pick a fight, what would be worth fighting for?

These aren't rhetorical questions. They're the foundation of everything that follows. Your answers will determine whether you build a brand that matters or a brand that just exists.

The War for Attention

Make no mistake: you are already in a war. Every day, your brand is competing for the most valuable resource in the modern economy: human attention. And you're not just competing against your direct competitors. You're competing against every notification, every meme, every piece of content fighting for the same eyeballs.

In that war, nice brands are bringing pillows to gunfights. They're showing up with good intentions and tasteful messaging while their competitors are launching psychological warfare disguised as marketing campaigns.

This book is your armory. Every chapter is a weapon. Every strategy is ammunition. Every case study is intelligence from the front lines of the attention war.

But here's the thing about weapons: they're only dangerous in the hands of someone brave enough to use them.

The Point of No Return

Once you understand beautiful brutality, once you see how polarization creates loyalty, how honesty builds empires, and how taking sides multiplies success, you can't unsee it. You'll watch vanilla brands die their quiet deaths and know exactly why. You'll see through the comfortable lies that keep most companies safely unsuccessful.

You'll also realize you have a choice: keep playing it safe until you're safely forgotten, or embrace the beautiful brutality that turns brands into movements, customers into evangelists, and businesses into legends.

The choice is yours. But choose quickly.

Every day you spend being nice is a day your competitors spend being memorable. Every campaign you launch to offend no one is a campaign your enemies launch to excite someone.

Your brand is already dying. The question is whether you'll resurrect it as something magnificent or let it die quietly like all the others.

Welcome to beautiful brutality. Your comfortable death ends here.

Now let's build something people can't help but pay attention to.

CHAPTER 1
Beautiful Brutality

Why "nice" brands die quietly

Here's a truth that'll make marketing executives choke on their kombucha: every "nice" brand is slowly committing suicide, and they're too polite to scream while they do it.

They bleed themselves out gently, smiling as they whisper, "We don't want to offend anyone," until they vanish into irrelevance. Meanwhile, the so-called "difficult" brands, the ones your mother would warn you about, are busy building empires, converting strangers into disciples, and laughing all the way to the bank.

Think about it: when's the last time you felt anything about a "nice" brand? When did vanilla ever make you cancel plans, skip meals, or tattoo a logo on your chest? Exactly. Never. Because nice is the kiss of death in an economy where attention is the most valuable currency and people are scrolling past your existence at light speed.

This chapter is about embracing **beautiful brutality**, the art of being honest with style, controversial with charm, and polarizing with purpose. By the end, you'll see why playing it safe is the most dangerous strategy of all, and why the brands you remember are the ones that made you feel something, even if that feeling started as hatred.

Ready to kill your inner people-pleaser? Let's get brutal.

The Problem with Playing Nice

Picture brand suicide in slow motion. It's 2012. JCPenney, America's sweetheart department store, decides to play really nice. Too nice.

Their bold new idea? Scrap sales, coupons, and "fake" discounts. Instead, offer simple, everyday low prices for everyone. No games. No gimmicks. Just fairness across the board. Sounds noble, right? Like something your kindergarten teacher would clap for?

It was a $985 million catastrophe. The company hemorrhaged 100,000 customers per day. Sales cratered 25% in one year. The CEO was gone faster than you can say "everyone is welcome."

Why? Because JCPenney forgot a fundamental truth of human psychology: **we don't want equality. We want to feel special.**

Their "fair" system stripped away everything that made shopping feel like a hunt. No more thrill of scoring 70% off.

No more pride in using a coupon. No more sense of beating the system. By trying to please everyone, they killed the magic for everyone.

Here's the brutal reality: when you try to offend no one, you excite no one. In trying to welcome all, they became invisible to all. Safety killed them faster than any competitor ever could.

Safety equals invisibility. Every time you choose the "safe" option, the bland message, the inoffensive logo, the "we're for everyone" positioning, you're whispering into a hurricane. You're bringing a pillow to a knife fight. You're showing up to a rock concert with a ukulele.

Why Outrage Hijacks Our Brains

Here's the dirty little neuroscience behind it: outrage is a performance-enhancing drug for attention. When something shocks us, an offensive ad, a savage tweet, a brand calling BS on an entire industry, it sparks a dopamine spike. That chemical hit feels electric. Our brains light up, our fight-or-flight reflex kicks in, and suddenly, we can't look away.

Outrage grabs the steering wheel of your attention and won't let go. That's why "nice" messages scroll by like wallpaper, while the brutal ones stop you mid-scroll, finger frozen, heart rate rising. Safe brands whisper; brutal brands trigger a full-body neurological response. And in a marketplace drowning in noise, the only way to be remembered is to hit the brain where it can't ignore you.

Nice brands aren't remembered. They aren't talked about. They don't get memed, debated, or worshipped. They just... exist. Quietly. Politely. Until they don't.

If nobody hates you by Tuesday, nobody will remember you by Friday.

Brutality = Honesty with Style

Before you start plotting your brand's villain era, let's be clear: **brutality isn't cruelty.** It's not about shock value or tossing out slurs to grab headlines. That's lazy.

Real brutality is raw honesty delivered with style. It's saying what everyone's thinking but no one dares to say. It's calling out industry BS while looking damn good doing it. It's being so unapologetically yourself that some people fall in love with you and others can't stand the sight of you.

Want proof? Look at Cards Against Humanity.

They built a billion-dollar empire on our darkest instincts. Our inappropriate jokes, our bad thoughts, and our guilty laughter. Their tagline? "A party game for horrible people."

Not "fun for the whole family." Not "bringing friends together." Not "wholesome entertainment." Nope. They called their customers horrible, and those customers lined up in droves. Finally, someone was honest about who we really are.

Cards Against Humanity didn't apologize. They didn't try to make everyone comfortable. Instead, they handed people a permission slip to unleash their inner terrible human for a night, and people worshipped them for it.

Their success wasn't despite the brutality. It was because of it. And the genius? They paired that dark honesty with sleek design, sharp copy, and clever marketing. They didn't just embrace the shadows; they made the shadows stylish.

Case Study: When Ugly Became a Superpower

Take Crocs. For years, they were the poster child of "safe," a clunky, practical shoe that your dentist wore on weekends. People mocked them. Fashionistas gagged. They were a punchline.

Then something wild happened: Crocs leaned into the ugly. Instead of chasing "nice" approval from the fashion world, they doubled down on their cartoonish absurdity. Bright colors. Meme-worthy collabs. Platform Crocs with literal spikes. They stopped apologizing and started saying: *Yeah, we're hideous. That's the point.*

The result? Sales exploded. They went from being the shameful shoe you hid in the closet to a $2 billion cultural phenomenon, embraced by Gen Z, celebrities, and even Balenciaga.

Because here's the formula:

- Brutality without style = being a jerk.
- Style without brutality = being forgettable.
- Brutality + style = **beautiful brutality.**

Charm + Controversy > Vanilla Safety

Most brands think they have to choose: be likable or polarizing. Charm or controversy.

Wrong. The truth? Charm amplifies controversy, and controversy makes charm unforgettable.

Think about the most interesting people you know. Are they the ones who always agree? Who never ruffle feathers? Who play it safe in every conversation? Hell no. The ones who stick in your head make you laugh, then make you think, then make you question everything.

Brands work the same way.

Look at Liquid Death Water. Half the world thinks they're genius. The other half thinks they're toxic. Everyone talks about them.

Their brutal truth: soda and energy drinks are poison, but water is boring. So they gave water the aesthetic of a metal band. Skull logo. Aggressive font. Tagline: "Murder your thirst."

Parents clutch pearls. Health nuts debate. Critics roll their eyes. And all of that controversy keeps the brand at the center of the conversation.

Meanwhile, every "safe" water brand is lost in the beige fog of "premium hydration." Liquid Death made people feel like rebels just for drinking water, and now they're worth $700 million.

The psychology is simple: attraction comes with repulsion. When you create something some people adore and others despise, you force everyone to pick a side. And sides drive loyalty.

Safe brands avoid this tension. They aim for universal appeal. But universal appeal is brand suicide. Switzerland doesn't have raving fans. It has polite tourists who visit once and forget.

Legends are born in the space between charm and controversy.

The Paradox of Love Through Offense

Here's the twist: the thing that first offends people often becomes the very thing they love most about you.

I call it the Howard Stern Effect.

For decades, Stern was branded a menace—crude, offensive, out of bounds. But studies showed his haters listened longer than his fans. Fans tuned in for 90 minutes. Haters? Two and a half hours.

Why? Because controversy demands attention. Offense forces focus. Once people are locked in, they start noticing the wit behind the crudeness, the intelligence under the shock value, the vulnerability beneath the bravado. Hatred morphs into obsession.

That's the paradox: sometimes, you have to offend people into loving you.

Safe brands never unlock that journey. They get polite nods that lead nowhere. Brutal brands get stories like, "I used to hate them; now I can't live without them." That's not failure; that's mastery.

Imagine a CEO running a startup that wanted to be everyone's best friend. Their product was bold, an AI-powered hiring tool that actually weeded out fluff résumés, but their messaging? Pure oatmeal. *"We make hiring easier for everyone."* Everyone? Really? That tagline could have belonged to a coffee maker.

They were terrified of saying the truth: that most résumés are garbage, and most hiring managers waste hours pretending otherwise. Instead of owning that brutal honesty, they tried to play nice, tiptoeing around the egos of job seekers.

The result? Crickets. No one remembered them, no one shared their story, and they bled money on ads that inspired zero emotion. Playing nice backfired. They blended into the beige wall of "helpful" HR software.

When they finally scrapped the fluff and led with the radical truth: *"Stop hiring liars with shiny résumés,"* suddenly people paid attention. Some hated it. But others loved it so much they begged for demos. That single line did more for them in two weeks than their "nice" messaging did in a year.

Your Brutality Drill

Enough theory; let's make this hurt a little. Grab a notebook and answer two questions:

1. In one sentence, where is your brand *too nice* right now? Maybe it's your tagline. Maybe it's the way you avoid naming competitors. Maybe it's the watered-down mission statement you cooked up to please the board. Write it down. No filters.
2. Now flip it: if you stripped away the nice and got brutally honest, what would you say instead? How would you describe your product if you were forbidden to use buzzwords? How would you position yourself if your job was to offend the right people?

That gap, the space between "too nice" and "brutally honest", is where your next breakthrough lives.

The Beautiful Truth

If this chapter made you squirm, good. Discomfort means you're paying attention.

Here's the beautiful truth: in a world where everyone is desperate to be liked, being unapologetically yourself is the most radical strategy of all.

Nice brands die because they never live loudly. They whisper when they should scream. They apologize when they should double down. They try to be everything to everyone and end up being nothing to anyone.

Brutal brands make the opposite choice. They choose honesty over harmony. Polarization over popularity. Memorability over mediocrity.

Because the opposite of love isn't hate; it's indifference. And indifference is the real killer.

So your brand has two choices: play it safe and die slowly, or embrace beautiful brutality and live forever in the minds of the people who matter.

The vanilla brands? They're already dead. The funeral starts tomorrow. Will you be in the coffin or giving the eulogy?

The question isn't whether you can afford to be brutal. It's whether you can afford not to be.

Welcome to beautiful brutality. Your boring brand just died, and something magnificent is about to be born.

CHAPTER 2

The Brand as a Weapon

Branding is not lipstick; it's a loaded gun

Let me demolish your sweet little illusion about branding: it's not pretty pictures and pastel palettes. You don't slap on a logo and call it a day. That's Instagram-filter thinking. While you're fumbling with font weights, your competitors are loading tactical nukes.

Branding is not cosmetic surgery. It's open-heart surgery. It's not decoration; it's ammunition. Every brand choice you make, every color, every word, every image, every public stance, is a bullet fired into the marketplace. And like real ammunition, intention doesn't matter much; impact does. A well-aimed brand decision creates allies who will fight for you. A misfired one creates enemies who will make it their mission to see you fail.

When the Shot Backfires

Not every bullet hits the right target. Remember Pepsi's infamous Kendall Jenner ad? The one where a can of soda supposedly solved police brutality and systemic injustice?

That wasn't branding; it was a misfire so loud it echoed through culture.

Pepsi wanted "unity." What they got was universal ridicule. The ad trivialized real pain, made activists look like props, and treated protest as a photo op. Instead of recruiting allies, they created enemies, not the useful kind. Pepsi didn't polarize; they patronized. That's the difference between weaponized branding and a clumsy cosplay of it.

The lesson? Brutality works when it's grounded in truth. When it's fake, forced, or tone-deaf, your weapon turns on you.

Brands that treat identity like décor show up to a gunfight with a makeup brush. The ones that win understand branding as a weapon: loaded with purpose, aimed with precision, and fired with confidence.

Why Branding Is Ammunition, Not Decoration

Here's the CMO truth no one says at the holiday dinner: your brand isn't there to make you feel warm and fuzzy. It exists to change behavior. Branding is behavioral engineering disguised as creative expression. It's psychology wrapped in packaging. Its job is to implant ideas so deeply that people start to believe they were their own.

Take Nike's Swoosh. That tiny curve is not a symbol for shoes. It's a cultural projectile launched into billions of minds each day. Every time you see it, you're not just reminded of footwear; you're cued into a whole identity: grit, rebellion, achievement, "Just Do It." That logo doesn't sell product; it sells the narrative of who you become wearing it.

Nike didn't get lucky. They weaponized perception. Ads, endorsements, and campaigns were bullets arranged into a single mission: when someone wants to be better, they think Nike. The Swoosh is tattooed on identities, not just textiles.

Here's the kicker: weapons polarize. For every person inspired by Nike, there's someone else who sees the Swoosh and recoils, corporatism, overpriced sneakers, exploitation. Nike doesn't try to please that person. They don't build for universal love. They build to be unforgettable.

Decoration sits on the surface. Ammunition goes deep. If your brand feels like tasteful interior design, it's because it's been designed to be forgettable. If your brand changes what people do and how they see themselves, congratulations; that's weaponized branding.

How to Aim Your Brand

Most brands don't aim. They spray and pray: broad campaigns, bland positioning, messages tossed everywhere like confetti. That approach makes noise but wastes ammunition.

Precision matters. Professional marksmen pick a target, steady their breath, and let one bullet do the work. Your brand needs that same ruthless accuracy.

Here's a simple framework to turn your brand into a precision weapon: the **Love/Hate Audience Map**. Do this now; grab a pen. Draw two columns: "MUST LOVE US" and "OKAY TO HATE US."

In "MUST LOVE US," be painfully specific. Not "millennials" or "professionals." Name real humans with real lives and real problems: Maria, 39, who juggles two jobs and wants something reliable; Jamal, 26, who values craftsmanship and will evangelize brands that honor it. The point is empathy sharpened into a target.

In "OKAY TO HATE US," be equally concrete. Not "people who don't like change." Name the attitudes and habits you are willing to alienate: the bargain hunter who worships the cheapest price above all else; the influencer who expects constant validation. If your "okay to hate us" list is empty, you have no aim.

Every legendary brand knows its enemy, some ideology, habit, or expectation it will challenge. That's not nastiness; it's focus. A sniper rifle is precise because it chooses a target. A shotgun sprays because it fears missing. Which are you?

When you know who you're aiming for and who you're willing to miss, every decision becomes simpler. Colors, copy, partnerships, product features, they're ammunition choices. Will this bullet hit my target or my non-target? If it hits the wrong people, it's working against you.

Aim with purpose or die by accident. There is no middle ground.

Your Targeting Worksheet

Take this beyond theory. Create two lists right now:

MUST LOVE US:

- Who are the exact people you need in your corner?
- What are their lives like? What do they obsess over? What would make them evangelize you?

OKAY TO HATE US:

- Who are you perfectly fine alienating?
- What beliefs, habits, or values do they hold that clash with yours?

Draw the line. Put names, attitudes, and even stereotypes on paper. If your lists feel too broad, you're not aiming; you're spraying. And spraying is how brands waste ammunition.

Polarize or Perish

The branding industry has dressed up cowardice as nuance. Strategy sessions turn into therapy: "Let's find our authentic voice." That's soft-sell nonsense. Strategy should be about picking a side and loading your ammunition accordingly.

Ben & Jerry's could have stayed in the flavor lane, new cones, seasonal swirls, cute tubs. Instead, they weaponized values: marriage equality, climate action, criminal justice reform. They knowingly pissed off half the aisle. Why risk sales over politics? Because in an attention-scarce world, neutrality is a luxury few brands can afford. Ben & Jerry's transformed ice cream into identity and earned an army of defenders who buy more than dessert. They buy a manifesto.

Strategic polarization is different from attention-seeking outrage. The former builds tribes; the latter builds enemies. Ben & Jerry's doesn't attack people; they attack systems. That phrasing lets supporters feel righteous without forcing opponents into personal humiliation. It's smart, effective, and profitable.

If your brand tries to appeal to everyone, it will appeal to no one. The graveyard of business is full of brands that tried to be neutral and ended up irrelevant. If you stand for nothing, you will die for nothing.

The Ethics of Pulling the Trigger

Weaponized branding is powerful, and power always tempts abuse. Some brands exploit outrage for cheap attention, baiting people into fights they never meant to finish. That's not bravery; that's manipulation.

There's a line between provocation and exploitation. Cross it, and you stop being a movement; you become a con. Brutal honesty works because it reveals something real. Weaponized lies destroy trust forever.

The responsible way to wield branding as a weapon is to attack systems, not victims; ideas, not vulnerable groups. Punch up, not down. Stand for something bigger than clicks. When you know exactly who you're fighting for and what you're fighting against, your brutality has integrity, and integrity is what makes it sustainable.

If No One Hates You, No One Loves You

Love and hate aren't opposites; they're cousins. The real opposite of both is indifference, and indifference kills brands.

Consider Chick-fil-A. In 2012, CEO comments on same-sex marriage lit a firestorm. Boycotts, protests, headlines. Chaos. Many brands would have apologized and folded. Chick-fil-A doubled down on core values, refused to pivot, and continued doing business as usual.

Result? Sales grew. Loyal customers admired the company's backbone; new customers discovered the product and service amid the noise. The controversy didn't bury them; it amplified them. Haters were suddenly the brand's unpaid marketing team, tracking every move and keeping the brand in the public eye.

The paradox: the people who pay the most attention to a brand are not always its fans. Sometimes they're its critics. But intense attention breeds familiarity, and familiarity can lead to affection. Brands that provoke deep reactions create the conditions for people to move from anger to advocacy.

Vanilla brands rarely trigger that arc. No one goes from "I don't care" to "I can't live without this" because indifference short-circuits emotional investment.

The goal isn't to manufacture hate. It's to be so unabashedly yourself that strong reactions are inevitable. Some will love you; some will hate you. Both will remember you and talk about you. Both will make your brand matter.

Lock and Load

We stand at the fork between ornament and ordnance. Your brand is already a weapon; the only questions are: are you aiming it, and do you have the courage to pull the trigger?

Every logo, tagline, color choice, product decision, and public stance is ammunition. There is no neutral ground.

Nike didn't become culture by making marginally better sneakers. Ben & Jerry's didn't build a movement with superior dairy. Chick-fil-A didn't get devotion strictly from chicken quality. They became legends by recognizing branding as behavioral warfare and by choosing their battles.

So stop treating identity like interior design. Stop asking your brand to be everyone's friend. Load with purpose. Aim with ruthless specificity. Fire with the confidence of a team that knows who they serve and who they're willing to miss.

Your competitors are still applying lipstick. You're loading ammunition. The question isn't whether branding is a weapon. The question is whether you have the nerve to use it.

Lock, load, and let your brand do the damage it was meant to do. Your targets are waiting.

Your Brand Manifesto

Write your brand manifesto as if it were a declaration of war. Be specific:

- **Who are you fighting for?** Name your allies, the people you exist to serve, defend, and empower.
- **Who are you fighting against?** Name the enemies: mediocrity, corruption, apathy, exploitation. Whatever forces you exist to dismantle.

- **What is your rallying cry?** Condense your mission into a line your tribe could shout in the streets.

This isn't copywriting fluff. This is a battle standard. Your manifesto should be so clear that your team, your customers, and your enemies know exactly what you stand for and what you'll never compromise on.

If branding is war, your manifesto is your declaration. Plant the flag. Draw the line. And let the world know where you stand.

CHAPTER 3

The Power of Polarization

Why beige is the most dangerous color

Let's rip off the bandage: **beige isn't neutral; it's neutered.** It's cowardice disguised as strategy. It's the sound of executives applauding themselves for "professionalism" while their brand is quietly lowered into the coffin of irrelevance.

Every time you choose beige, whether in your visuals, your messaging, or your positioning, you're not reducing risk. You're ensuring death. It's brand suicide on a slow drip. And the worst part? You convince yourself you're doing the "smart" thing.

Business school taught you to minimize risk, appeal broadly, and keep things clean and safe. But here's the brutal truth: in a world where consumers face **10,000 marketing messages a day**, "safe" is the same as "nonexistent." Whispering is not restraint. Whispering is invisibility.

The brands that thrive don't avoid division; they wield it. They treat polarization as a weapon, not a weakness. They know that being loved by some and hated by others is not a liability. It's an edge. It's fuel.

Because here's the math that terrifies beige brands: 50% love + 50% hate is infinitely stronger than 100% indifference.

So ask yourself right now: when was the last time your brand provoked a strong emotion—love, loyalty, anger, obsession? If you can't remember, that silence is the sound of a brand already in hospice care.

Love and hate are both engagement. Both are passion. Both are proof you matter. Indifference? Indifference is the black hole that swallows entire companies.

This chapter is about turning polarization into your sharpest strategic tool, not something you stumble into, but something you build with intent. It's time to bury the fantasy of Switzerland neutrality. **Neutrality doesn't save brands; it sterilizes them.**

The Beige Brand Graveyard

Step into the most depressing cemetery in capitalism: **The Beige Brand Graveyard.**

It's crowded with companies that played it "safe." Brands that spent millions to be inoffensive and ended up irrelevant. Their epitaphs all read the same: *"They tried to appeal to everyone. They were remembered by no one."*

Take **Blockbuster Video.** They weren't hated. They weren't loved. They were... fine. And then they were gone.

Blockbuster had all the cards: thousands of locations, millions of customers, industry dominance. When Netflix came along with their mail-order DVD experiment, half the market scoffed. *"Who wants to wait days for a movie when you can drive to the store?"* The other half thought it was revolutionary. *"Why drive anywhere when movies can come to me?"*

Netflix didn't waste ammo trying to win over the skeptics. They ignored them. They built for the believers. They leaned into the polarizing bet that convenience would beat habit.

Blockbuster, meanwhile, beige'd themselves to death. They held meetings. They ran focus groups. They studied charts. And they decided, get this, that customers "weren't ready" for change.

Netflix didn't need customers to be "ready." They needed them to be curious. And once curiosity turned into habit, loyalty was born.

Result? Blockbuster filed for bankruptcy. Netflix became a $240 billion juggernaut that rewrote entertainment itself. Beige wasn't just bad; it was the very thing that gave Netflix the oxygen to dominate.

Are You Beige?

Answer these yes/no questions. If you say "yes" more than twice, grab a shovel; you're digging your brand's grave.

- Do all your competitors' websites look suspiciously similar to yours?
- Could your tagline be swapped with theirs and no one would notice?
- Do you describe yourself as "innovative," "reliable," or "trusted partner"?
- Are your ads designed to "offend no one"?
- Does your social media sound like a polite intern wrote it?
- Have you ever delayed a bold idea because someone in leadership said, "But what if people don't like it?"

If you're nodding along, congratulations, you're beige. And beige is terminal.

Walk further into the graveyard and you'll trip over giants: **Circuit City, Borders, Sears, RadioShack.** Entire empires reduced to corpses because they mistook broad appeal for relevance.

Beige brands don't just die quietly. They die while handing victory to the bold.

The most dangerous color in branding isn't loud red, aggressive black, or radioactive neon. **It's beige, because beige is the color of surrender.**

Love vs. Hate Rivalries

Now, let's leave the graveyard and step onto the battlefield, where brands with backbone turn polarization into an engine of loyalty.

Think **Apple vs. Android.** This isn't about phones. It's about tribes. Apple is simplicity, exclusivity, *"it just works."* Android is freedom, customization, *"don't be a sheep."* Each side sees the other as fundamentally misguided.

And that's the point.

Apple didn't build compatibility bridges to win everyone over. They built walls. Beautiful, frustrating, polarizing walls. Proprietary chargers. Locked ecosystems. Exclusive apps. Every choice was gasoline on the rivalry fire.

Apple users defend their loyalty with near-religious fervor. Android users defend their independence with equal passion. The fight itself makes both sides stronger. Nobody shrugs about Apple vs. Android. They argue. They evangelize. They recruit.

Same story: **Coke vs. Pepsi, Nike vs. Adidas, PlayStation vs. Xbox, Tesla vs. legacy automakers.** Even Salesforce built its empire by polarizing against "traditional CRM dinosaurs," while beige competitors faded into irrelevance.

The genius of polarization is that it taps into tribal psychology older than civilization. Humans define themselves not just by who they are but by who they oppose. Brands that recognize this aren't just selling products; they're arming identities.

When your customer sees your competitor's logo and thinks, *"That's the enemy,"* you're no longer in the business of selling things. You're in the business of building armies.

If your brand doesn't have enemies, it doesn't have identity.

Polarization Beyond the Usual Suspects

It's not just Western giants playing this game. In India, Reliance Jio flipped an entire telecom industry by going scorched earth on pricing. Free calls. Dirt-cheap data. Competitors mocked them as reckless, unsustainable, even suicidal. But Jio turned outrage into dominance, forcing the market to bend to their model. Today, they control over 400 million subscribers, and the rivals who laughed are either dead or begging for scraps.

Or look at Nando's in South Africa. Their ads don't play safe. They lampoon politicians, jab at cultural taboos, and stir conversations that make executives sweat. The result?

They're not just selling chicken; they're embedding themselves in national identity. People talk about their ads as much as their food. They provoke, they polarize, and they profit.

Emerging markets remind us: polarization isn't a Western luxury; it's a universal law of attention.

Hatred Is Proof of Life

Let me tell you something that will make your PR department hyperventilate: **the real metric of brand vitality isn't how many people love you. It's how many people care enough to feel anything at all.**

Because hatred, real, obsessive, noisy hatred, is proof of relevance. It means you've carved deep enough into culture that people can't ignore you, even when they want to.

Look at **Elon Musk**.

Half the world crowns him a visionary. The other half calls him a reckless egomaniac. Almost no one is neutral. And that polarization is his greatest asset.

Musk gets mentioned in the press nearly nine times more than any other CEO. Over half of that comes from critics. His haters literally subsidize his PR.

Every controversy, tweet, lawsuit, rocket explosion only amplifies him. His critics dissect his every move, keeping him perpetually in the spotlight. And here's the paradox: the longer they pay attention, the more they're forced to watch his wins. Rockets land. Cars improve. Stock prices rise. Some critics, unwillingly, become converts.

Tesla spends **$0** on advertising. Zero. Their marketing department is Elon Musk being polarizing on Twitter. Meanwhile, legacy auto companies hemorrhage billions on beige commercials that vanish from memory in five seconds.

Musk proves a fundamental law of the attention economy: being hated is often more profitable than being ignored.

And here's the brutal truth: if no one has ever said they hate your brand, then no one has ever loved it either.

When Polarization Crosses the Line

Polarization is a weapon, but misfire, and you don't just miss the target; you shoot yourself in the foot.

Remember United Airlines' infamous "dragging incident"? The video of a bloodied passenger went viral, and instead of standing for firm values, United looked like bullies weaponizing their brand against their own customers. That wasn't bold. It was brand suicide in slow motion.

Or think of brands that lean too hard into political division, clumsily using outrage as clickbait. They don't polarize with purpose; they just polarize for attention. And attention without alignment is toxic. It erodes trust, sparks boycotts, and leaves scars that even billion-dollar ad budgets can't heal.

The takeaway? Polarization is powerful when it's strategic. Push it too far, and you become a cautionary tale instead of a legend.

How to Craft Division Without Destruction

Before you run off and troll your own customers, let's get disciplined. **Polarization without strategy is self-immolation. Polarization with purpose is empire-building.**

Here's how to do it right:

1. Polarize on values, not people

Don't call your customers stupid. Attack the system, not the individual. Tesla doesn't insult drivers. They attack fossil fuels. Ben & Jerry's doesn't attack conservatives. They attack unjust policies. People can disagree with your ideas today and join you tomorrow. But if you attack them personally, they'll never come back.

2. Make your enemy bigger than your competition

Don't waste bullets on rivals. Make your fight about concepts. Apple didn't just battle Microsoft; they battled ugly, clunky design. Nike doesn't fight Adidas; they fight mediocrity itself. The bigger the enemy, the bigger the movement.

3. Give people something to join, not just something to hate

Polarization without identity is just negativity. Patagonia isn't just against environmental destruction; they're for authentic adventure. Tesla isn't just anti-gas; they're pro-future. Define the "yes" as much as the "no."

4. Stay consistent, even when it costs you

Anyone can be bold when it's profitable. Real credibility is built when you hold your position through backlash. Nike with Kaepernick. Ben & Jerry's with climate activism. Chick-fil-A with values. The staying power of your stance matters more than the stance itself.

5. Monitor the health of your polarization

Polarization works when passion runs both ways. Lovers and haters both screaming your name. It fails when the haters are louder than your fans. Track both sides. Balance matters.

6. Escalate or de-escalate intentionally

Not every firestorm deserves gasoline. Sometimes you double down. Sometimes you go silent. The skill is knowing when polarization is productive tension and when it's destructive chaos.

Remember: polarization is not a tantrum. It's a scalpel. Used carefully, it cuts through the noise. Used recklessly, it just makes you bleed out.

Choose Your Battle

The beige brand graveyard is overflowing with companies that mistook neutrality for strategy. They were buried under their own politeness.

But the hall of fame? That's reserved for the brands that picked fights. Apple chose design over compatibility. Tesla chose the future over tradition. Ben & Jerry's chose values over neutrality.

What does your brand believe so strongly that you'd risk losing customers for it? If you don't have an answer, you don't have a brand; you have beige wallpaper waiting to peel.

Do this right now: Google your brand + "love." Then Google your brand + "hate." If nothing comes up, congratulations, you're not polarizing. You're irrelevant.

Here's the truth: you don't get to choose *whether* to polarize. Every brand that matters eventually does. The only choice you get is whether to polarize strategically, authentically, and powerfully, or to stumble into irrelevance by accident.

The middle ground is quicksand. Pick a side. Build an army.

Beige brands end up in the graveyard. Polarizing brands end up in the history books. Which destiny are you choosing?

Your Polarization Drill

Write two opposing customer reviews of your brand:

Glowing Review:

"They *get me*. They don't just sell a product—they fight for people like me. I'd tattoo their logo on my arm if my mom wouldn't disown me."

Scathing Review:

"They're arrogant. Overpriced. Offensive. I can't stand what they stand for."

Now step back. What do these extremes reveal? Do the haters make the lovers' loyalty stronger? Does the scorn confirm your edge? If both reviews feel plausible, congratulations, you're not beige. You're alive, dangerous, and unforgettable.

CHAPTER 4
Charm Is a Weapon Too

Disarm before you detonate

Here's where most people completely misinterpret the philosophy of beautiful brutality: they think it's all about the brutality.

They read the first three chapters, get high on polarization adrenaline, and march into the market swinging their opinions like a berserk Viking with a battle axe. They attack everything. They antagonize everyone. They burn every bridge in sight. Then they sit among the ashes and wonder why no one is celebrating their "authenticity."

Then they scratch their heads and say, "Why did my authentic brand crash and burn?"

Here's why: because **the most dangerous weapons aren't the obvious ones.** The Trojan Horse wasn't terrifying; it was a gift. The deadliest assassins in history weren't foaming-at-the-mouth killers; they were the charming guests who made you laugh at dinner before slipping something fatal into your wine.

Brutality without charm isn't bravery. It's stupidity. And stupidity doesn't build brands; it buries them.

When Brutality Backfires

Imagine a CMO whose edgy rebrand tanked. A conversation with the boss might go something like this:

Boss: "What happened?"
CMO: "We came out swinging. Called our competitors idiots. Called customers sheep. Launched a campaign with all the subtlety of a Molotov cocktail."
Boss: "And the result?"
CMO: *sighs* "We were right. But nobody cared because nobody liked us."
Boss: "So what changed?"
CMO: "We added charm. Same brutal truths, but wrapped in wit, humor, and a wink. People laughed first and then agreed with us."

That's the shift most leaders miss: the truth lands harder when people *want* you to win.

The brands that win at this game understand something the reckless ones miss: **you have to disarm people before you can detonate their assumptions.** You have to seduce them into listening before you shock them into thinking. You have to make them like you before you force them to choose you over the competition.

Charm is the Trojan Horse that gets you past the gatekeepers. It lowers defenses. It sneaks past cynicism. It buys you the space to be polarizing. Once you're inside the walls, once people are laughing, engaged, and paying attention, that's when you can deploy your brutal payload.

This isn't manipulation. This is seduction. And seduction is older, stronger, and more effective than any marketing framework you've ever been taught.

The brands that master charm and brutality together don't just win market share. They win cultural share. They don't just create customers. They create accomplices. They don't just make sales. They make legends.

Time to learn how to smile while you stab the status quo.

Charm as the Trojan Horse

The most beautiful corporate executions don't always happen in boardrooms or ad campaigns. Sometimes they happen in 280 characters.

Case in point: Wendy's on Twitter.

Most fast-food chains treated social media like a corporate safety pamphlet with emojis. Polite updates about menu items. PR-approved customer service replies. Messages so bland you'd forget them while reading them.

Wendy's showed up with a flamethrower, and then did something brilliant: they wrapped that flamethrower in charm.

They weren't just aggressive. They were witty, sharp, and self-aware. They roasted competitors with lines so clever people begged to be targeted. They insulted customers with such humor that the "victims" proudly shared screenshots of their humiliation. Getting burned by Wendy's became a badge of honor.

When a random user accused them of serving frozen beef, Wendy's didn't roll out a lifeless press release. They replied: *"Sorry to hear you think that, but you're wrong. blocks user."*

When Carter Wilkerson asked how many retweets he'd need for a year of free nuggets, they said "18 million," a ridiculous number. But when he came close, they rewarded him anyway, turning the stunt into the most retweeted tweet in history.

Wendy's Twitter became entertainment first, advertising second. People followed not because they loved the food, but because they loved the voice. They checked the account like it was their favorite late-night show. Competitors became punchlines. Fans became amplifiers.

The result? Sales climbed. Brand value skyrocketed. Their snarky Twitter voice generated more earned media than multi-million-dollar ad buys. And it all worked because they led with charm.

If Wendy's had gone in guns blazing, just attacking without wit, just insulting without humor, they'd have been dismissed as angry and abrasive. But because the humor was clever, because the delivery was fun, people *wanted* to spread the destruction.

That's the Trojan Horse strategy: lead with entertainment, then smuggle your brutal truth inside the laughter.

The Science of Seduction

Why does charm work so well? Because the brain is wired for it.

Here's the science: **emotions drive decisions first; logic justifies them second.** The limbic system, the emotional core of the brain, processes information five times faster than the rational neocortex. People decide how they *feel* about you before they even realize they're deciding.

That means the first thing you must win is not agreement; it's affection. Not conviction; it's attention. And charm hijacks that process.

Take **Dollar Shave Club's legendary launch video.**

While Gillette droned on about blades, precision engineering, and "comfort strips," Dollar Shave Club's CEO, Mike Dubin, walked into a warehouse with a machete and said: *"Our blades are f**ing great."*

In under 90 seconds, he mocked industry giants, dropped irreverent jokes, smashed conventional messaging, and made people laugh so hard they clicked "buy" before they finished the video.

That wasn't logic. That was seduction.

Viewers didn't sit there rationally comparing blades per cartridge. They joined because they liked Mike. They wanted to be part of the rebellion. The charm slipped past their defenses and made them complicit in the destruction of an industry.

The outcome? Twenty-six million views in three months. Twelve thousand customers in 48 hours. A billion-dollar acquisition within four years.

Not because the blades were better. Because the story was better, and the story was irresistible because it was charming.

Charm bypasses resistance. It makes people lower their shields. It makes them *want* to spread your message because it entertains them. And once they've let you in, you can plant the brutal truth that tears down your competitors.

That's the science of seduction: charm makes customers agree with you before they even realize they're doing it.

Charm the Curious, Polarize the Committed

Now let's get strategic. Not everyone in your market should get the same treatment. Your audience falls into three critical groups:

The Curious. They're on the fence. Not enemies, but not committed. You don't bulldoze them; you charm them. Wit, humor, personality. Make them smile. Make them pay attention. Once they're relaxed and open, you can show them the full power of your convictions.

The Committed. These are your believers. They don't need charm; they need ammunition. They're your army. Give them clarity, conviction, and polarizing truths they can rally behind.

The Critics. These are your opponents. Here's where you play the double game: charm them into paying attention, then polarize hard enough to make them pick a side. You don't convert all of them, but you make them respect you, obsess over you, and amplify you.

Ryan Reynolds with Aviation Gin is the perfect case study.

He could've gone sleek and serious. Instead, he went self-aware, absurd, and hilarious. Curious people who had no intention of buying gin watched his ads because they were entertaining. Committed fans became evangelists, sharing everything he posted. Critics who thought celebrity alcohol was a cynical cash grab ended up talking about Aviation constantly, unintentionally spreading the message.

The charm was never separate from the brutality. It was the delivery system for it. Every joke doubled as a stab at industry conventions. Every absurd commercial made serious competitors look more ridiculous. Reynolds didn't just sell gin; he demolished the industry playbook with a smile.

Result? Aviation Gin's value exploded by 2,700% in just two years.

That's what happens when you charm the curious, polarize the committed, and make your critics unwilling amplifiers.

The Charm–Brutality Balance Scale

Picture a scale with charm on one side and brutality on the other. Here's how it works:

- **Too much charm, not enough brutality:** You're entertaining but forgettable. The audience laughs, then leaves.

- **Too much brutality, no charm:** You're abrasive. People flinch, then flee.
- **The sweet spot:** Just enough charm to disarm, just enough brutality to detonate. The laugh opens the door; the truth knocks it off its hinges.

Your job isn't to max out one side; it's to balance both until the delivery is irresistible and unforgettable.

Seductive Destruction

Here's the final truth about charm: it isn't the opposite of brutality. It's the amplifier.

Wendy's didn't just mock competitors; they made the audience *want* to be part of the roast. Dollar Shave Club didn't just attack razor companies; they made people laugh while cheering for the attack. Ryan Reynolds didn't just lampoon gin marketing; he turned mockery into millions.

Charm is the sugar that makes the poison taste sweet.

The Trojan Horse didn't succeed because it was strong; it succeeded because it looked harmless. That's what charm does: it disguises your most devastating strikes as gifts.

But here's the warning: charm must be authentic. Fake charm reeks. Corporate-approved humor feels like karaoke sung by robots. Customers smell it instantly. Once they detect insincerity, your Trojan Horse collapses into a dead horse.

The brands that succeed don't fake it; they risk. They dare. They're funny because the people behind them are funny. They're charming because the personality is real. Authenticity fuels charm, and charm fuels destruction.

Most brands fail here because they're too boring to be charming and too scared to be brutal. They end up stranded in the beige wasteland, entertaining no one, offending no one, remembered by no one.

But you? You won't make that mistake. You'll seduce before you strike. You'll charm before you polarize. You'll make your audience fall for you and then make them fight for you.

Because charm without brutality is entertainment. Brutality without charm is aggression. But charm plus brutality? That's cultural warfare disguised as comedy. That's seductive destruction.

The Mechanics of Humor in Branding

Want to weaponize charm? Use the oldest tricks in comedy:

- **Surprise:** Take the expected phrase and derail it. ("Our competitors say they're innovative. Cute. So is a Roomba.")

- **Exaggeration:** Blow the truth up to absurd proportions. ("We're not just cheaper; we're insultingly cheaper.")
- **Callbacks:** Reference your own jokes later so the audience feels in on the game. ("Remember when we said we were insultingly cheaper? Yeah, still true.")

These aren't gimmicks; they're tactical tools. Humor is memory glue. Pair it with your brutal truth, and people won't just hear it; they'll repeat it.

Rules of Seductive Destruction

1. **Lead with humor, follow with truth.** Make them laugh first, then make them think.
2. **Punch up, never down.** Attack broken systems, lazy competitors, or outdated norms, not vulnerable people.
3. **Make charm your camouflage.** Wrap your brutal message in entertainment so people welcome it instead of rejecting it.
4. **Don't fake it.** Authentic charm requires risk. If you sanitize it, you kill it.
5. **Escalate strategically.** Use charm to earn permission. Then unleash your polarizing convictions when it counts.
6. **Charm isn't optional.** It's the price of entry. Brutality alone is brutality. Brutality plus charm is unforgettable.

Smile Before You Strike

Here's the paradox of power: smiles are deadlier than scowls. Charm is the weapon that opens the door. Brutality is the explosion that follows.

The brands that change industries don't separate the two. They seduce while they stab. They disarm while they demolish. They entertain while they eviscerate.

Wendy's charmed the internet into cheering for their roasts. Dollar Shave Club seduced millions into destroying the razor industry. Ryan Reynolds turned gin mockery into billions.

They proved the rule: Disarm before you detonate.

Your smile is your Trojan Horse. Your humor is your disguise. Your authenticity is the gift that gets you through the gates. And once you're inside, that's when you let the brutality rip.

Charm is not weakness. Charm is the sharpest weapon you'll ever wield.

Your Charm Drill

Write three one-liners your brand could use to soften the blow before delivering a brutal truth. Here are examples to spark yours:

1. "We love you enough to tell you this might sting."
2. "Grab a helmet; we're about to be honest."
3. "Think of this as tough love, with extra emphasis on the tough."

Charm opens the door. Brutality makes the message unforgettable. Together, they turn your brand into the guest everyone can't stop talking about after the party.

CHAPTER 5

Ugly Truths, Beautiful Stories

Confessionals beat perfection

Here's the truth that makes agencies nervous, CMOs sweat, and CEOs reach for their stress toys: **your customers can smell bullshit from three quarterly reports away.**

Every glossy campaign, every polished product video, every brand film where employees beam like Stepford robots, it all screams the same thing: *"We're lying to you, and we're not even good at hiding it."*

People aren't idiots. They know your company isn't flawless. They know your employees don't wake up whistling corporate hymns. They know your product has cracks, quirks, and compromises. They know your CEO doesn't roll out of bed every morning whispering, *"I live to serve stakeholders today."*

So why do you keep pretending?

Because someone, somewhere, probably wearing a $3,000 suit and billing $750 an hour, sold you on the idea that

perfection sells. That showing weakness would make customers doubt you. That admitting flaws would break trust. That vulnerability would sink your share price.

That consultant was wrong. Dead wrong.

Here's reality: perfection is forgettable. Confession is unforgettable.

The brands that thrive in today's attention economy are not the ones hiding scars; they're the ones flaunting them. They don't polish themselves into sterile mannequins. They bleed in public. They own their flaws. They admit ugly truths and wrap them in stories so powerful customers can't look away.

Because people don't fall in love with your victories; they fall in love with your battles.

This chapter is about why flaws convert better than features, why vulnerability is your sharpest weapon, and why the most powerful sentence in business might be: *"We're human, and here's what that looks like."*

Time to stop lying beautifully and start telling ugly truths that build beautiful stories.

Why Features Don't Convert, Stories Do

Here's the myth that's been embalming brands for decades: **the belief that rational people make rational choices based on rational information.**

Every corporate PowerPoint is built on this fantasy. Bullet points about "unique value propositions." Charts comparing specs. Graphs showing performance advantages. Entire ad campaigns boasting about "new features" no one asked for.

But here's the reality: features don't convert. Stories do.

Features tell me what your product does. Stories tell me who I become when I use it. Features live in the brain. Stories live in the bloodstream.

Want proof? Look at Patagonia's "Don't Buy This Jacket" campaign.

On Black Friday 2011, when every brand was screaming "BUY MORE!", Patagonia took out a full-page ad in *The New York Times* with a simple headline: *"DON'T BUY THIS JACKET."*

Underneath, they confessed the ugly truth: making that jacket burned 20 pounds of carbon, wasted 135 liters of water, and created enough waste to choke a landfill. They begged customers to think twice before buying.

It was corporate heresy. Consultants called it retail suicide.

And yet Patagonia's sales jumped 30% that year. The campaign generated $10 million in earned media. Customers didn't just buy jackets; they bought into an identity: *"I'm the kind of person who thinks before I consume."*

The ugly truth, consumption is killing the planet, became the beautiful story: buying Patagonia means aligning with environmental conscience.

Patagonia whispered one confession while every other outdoor brand screamed the same promotion. And the whisper won.

Features fade. Stories stick. Nike doesn't sell "Air technology." They sell the story of grit and pushing past limits. Tesla doesn't sell "400-mile range." They sell the story of driving into the future. Apple doesn't sell megapixels; they sell the story of creativity and belonging to a tribe of innovators.

If you're still leading with specs, you're still selling like it's 1997. In today's economy, features don't sell products; stories sell identities.

Vulnerability: The Sharpest Weapon in Branding

Let's talk about the power most brands are too afraid to use: **vulnerability.**

When a friend admits their struggles, you don't think less of them; you feel closer to them. You don't lose respect; you gain intimacy. You don't see weakness; you see honesty.

The same principle applies to brands. But 99% of companies are too cowardly to test it. They'd rather look perfect and be ignored than admit flaws and be remembered.

Elon Musk refused to play that game.

In 2018, Tesla was in chaos. They were missing production targets. They were burning cash like a bonfire. Analysts were predicting bankruptcy. Most CEOs would have unleashed a polished PR campaign filled with "confidence in the future" nonsense.

Musk went on Twitter and confessed: *"Tesla is bleeding money like crazy. Production hell. Probably the most excruciating year of my life."*

He didn't hide the mess. He narrated it.

And something wild happened: customers didn't run. They leaned in. They defended Tesla in forums. They stuck out long waits for their Model 3 deliveries. They saw themselves in Musk's exhaustion.

His vulnerability turned customers into soldiers.

By admitting the pain, he made the mission feel bigger. By confessing the mess, he made the victories sweeter. When Tesla finally hit production milestones, the success felt personal, not just to Musk, but to the thousands of customers who had followed the struggle.

Tesla's stock rose 400% during its so-called "production hell." Meanwhile, Ford smiled through perfect PR and flatlined.

The brutal truth: perfection creates distance. Struggle creates intimacy.

Real vulnerability isn't dumping every failure on the table. That's therapy, not branding. Strategic vulnerability is about showing the scars that make your mission matter.

Formula: Struggle + Perseverance + Outcome = Story Worth Buying.

Customers don't want perfect companies. They want human companies. They don't want flawless myths. They want flawed fighters who overcome.

Your scars are your sales pitch.

Why Vulnerability Works in the Brain

This isn't just feel-good philosophy; it's biology. Neuroscience shows that when people witness genuine vulnerability, the brain releases oxytocin, the bonding hormone. It's the same chemical that floods a parent holding their newborn or a friend comforting another through heartbreak.

That hit of oxytocin makes people trust you more. It lowers their defenses. It rewires their brains to see you not as a faceless company, but as part of their tribe. Vulnerability is sticky because it isn't logic; it's chemistry.

So when your brand admits, "We screwed up," customers don't just nod. Their brains literally make them want to believe you. Perfection doesn't trigger oxytocin. Honesty does.

Embarrass Your Mother

Here's the litmus test for whether your marketing is bold enough: **If your campaign wouldn't embarrass your mother, it's probably too safe.**

Not because you should be vulgar, but because honesty so raw, so unpolished, so nakedly human usually makes polite people deeply uncomfortable.

Most campaigns are designed to make executives proud and mothers nod approvingly. That's why most campaigns are as memorable as elevator music.

Dove chose to embarrass everyone.

For decades, beauty brands trafficked in lies: perfect models, airbrushed skin, unattainable bodies. They made women hate themselves and then sold them overpriced hope.

Dove detonated the system. They ran the "Real Beauty" campaign featuring real women, different bodies, different ages, different skin. Wrinkles. Stretch marks. Imperfections.

They confessed the ugly truth: *"The beauty industry is lying to you."*

Executives were horrified. Competitors sneered. Mothers raised on glossy perfection clutched their pearls.

And customers? They wept with relief. Finally, a brand said what everyone knew but no one admitted. Finally, a brand celebrated instead of shamed.

Sales skyrocketed 700% over the next decade. Dove didn't just sell soap; they sold rebellion. They sold liberation from an industry addicted to lies.

The ugly truth, beauty marketing is toxic, became the beautiful story: real beauty is real people.

Case Study: When Small Brands Go Ugly

Take Oatly. Before they were a global dairy-free juggernaut, they were a scrappy Swedish brand trying to elbow into a milk-dominated market. Their ads didn't brag about features. Instead, they slapped up billboards with lines like: *"It's like milk, but made for humans."*

That brutal honesty offended the dairy lobby so much that lawsuits followed. Instead of hiding, Oatly printed the lawsuit in their ads, turning legal threats into proof of rebellion.

Customers didn't just buy oat milk; they bought the thrill of sticking it to Big Dairy. The ugly truth, cow's milk isn't for everyone, became a movement.

If your campaign could double as a polite holiday card, it's worthless. The marketing that matters embarrasses someone comfortable while liberating someone desperate.

Stop aiming for polite applause. Start aiming for emotional electricity.

Scars Sell Better Than Shine

Here's the liberating conclusion: **your flaws are not liabilities. They're assets.**

Patagonia confessed its environmental guilt. Tesla confessed its production hell. Dove confessed its industry's lies. Each confession became an unforgettable differentiator.

Meanwhile, their competitors polished their lies, ran beige campaigns, and quietly faded into irrelevance.

Your scars are your sales tools. Your failures are your features. Your confessions are your competitive edge.

Think about your favorite brands. They aren't the ones that looked perfect. They're the ones that fought, bled, admitted, struggled, and came out the other side with stories that made you feel human, not sold to.

The brands brave enough to bleed in public? Those are the brands customers would die for.

The Confession Framework

Here's your practical blueprint for turning ugly truths into beautiful stories:

1. **Identify your scars.** Write down the three biggest struggles your company has faced in the last five years. No polishing. No spin. Just raw scars.
2. **Find the universal struggle.** What's the human truth behind those scars? Missed deadlines = feeling overwhelmed. Failed launches = fear of being irrelevant. Overwork = guilt about balance. Universal truths are what connect.
3. **Confess selectively.** Choose one ugly truth you can admit without self-destruction. Don't dump everything. Pick the truth that magnifies your mission.
4. **Wrap it in story.** Don't just state the flaw. Frame it as part of the journey: struggle → perseverance → outcome.
5. **Make it the customer's story.** Position the confession not just as your truth, but as a mirror for your customer's reality. Invite them to see themselves in your scars.
6. **Turn it into a movement.** Create messaging that makes buying from you feel like joining a cause. Not

"buy our product," but "stand with us in this messy fight."

That's how you turn confessions into conversions.

Storytelling Drill: Flip Failure into Heroism

Grab a notebook and work through this exercise:

1. **Name the Failure.** Pick a major stumble your brand endured. Missed deadline, failed launch, brutal review. Write it down in plain, ugly detail.
2. **Find the Struggle.** Translate it into a universal human truth. Maybe it's about burnout, being underestimated, or trying something too bold too soon.
3. **Reframe the Arc.** Rewrite the failure as a heroic journey:
   o *The Flaw:* What went wrong.
   o *The Fight:* How you clawed your way through it.
   o *The Hook:* How the scar makes you stronger, wiser, or more trustworthy today.
4. **Tell It Out Loud.** If it makes you squirm, good; it means it's human.

Your ugliest story is usually your most magnetic.

Bleed in Public, Win in Private

So here we are, at the end of the confession booth. Let's recap the beautiful brutality of truth:

- **Perfection is sterile. Confession is magnetic.**
- **Features fade. Stories scar.**
- **Vulnerability isn't weakness. It's intimacy.**
- **Embarrassment is a sign you're being human, not beige.**
- **Scars outsell shine, every single time.**

Your competitors are still polishing their perfect smiles, hiding their flaws, and hoping no one notices the cracks.

You're going to do something different. You're going to bleed in public. You're going to confess strategically. You're going to tell ugly truths wrapped in beautiful stories.

Because your customers don't want another perfect brand to buy from. They want a human brand to believe in.

The ones who bleed out loud are the ones who live forever in loyalty.

So confess. Scar. Struggle. Embarrass your mother. Make someone uncomfortable. Make someone else cry with relief. Make your audience whisper: *"Finally, someone's telling the truth."*

Beautiful lies are forgettable. Ugly truths are unforgettable.

Time to weaponize yours.

Your Confession Drill

Tell a story about a major failure your brand endured. Maybe it was a product that flopped, a campaign that faceplanted, or a moment you thought you wouldn't recover.

Now rewrite it as a heroic journey where the flaw becomes the hook:

- The product didn't fail; it revealed what customers really wanted.
- The campaign didn't bomb; it exposed the gap in your strategy that you've since fixed.
- The near-collapse didn't ruin you; it forged loyalty from the people who stuck around.

Failures don't repel people. Sanitized lies do. Own the scar, tell the story, and let the flaw become the magnet.

CHAPTER 6

Create Villains, Crown Heroes

Every brand needs an enemy

Here's a storytelling truth that will revolutionize how you think about branding: **Your brand is boring because it has no enemies. Every legendary company in history built its empire by declaring war on something bigger than itself, and you're still playing patty-cake with the status quo.**

Not a competitor; that's small thinking. Not another company; that's boring thinking. I'm talking about a proper villain: a system, a mindset, an industry standard, a cultural norm that your brand exists to fight against.

Without a villain, there are no heroes. Without heroes, there are no legends.

Think about every story that ever mattered to you. Every movie that made you cheer, every book that made you care, every cause that made you donate money or time or emotional energy. I guarantee there was a villain, some force of evil, ignorance, or indifference that the hero had to overcome.

Your customers don't just want to buy products. They want to join crusades.

They want to feel like their purchase decisions matter for something bigger than their personal convenience. They want to believe that choosing your brand over the alternatives makes them part of the solution instead of part of the problem.

But you can't be the solution if you don't define the problem. You can't be the hero if you don't identify the villain.

Most brands are terrified of making enemies. They want to be Switzerland, neutral, inoffensive, acceptable to everyone. What they don't understand is that Switzerland doesn't have passionate fans. Switzerland has polite tourists who visit once and forget it exists.

Most brands are so afraid of offending anyone that they end up inspiring no one. They'd rather be Switzerland than Sparta, forgetting that nobody dies for neutral countries.

Heroes have enemies. Legends have wars. And wars create the strongest loyalty imaginable.

This chapter is about identifying your brand's villain, manufacturing productive conflict, and positioning yourself as the hero your customers have been waiting for. By the end, you'll understand why the brands people die for are always fighting against something bigger than themselves.

Time to pick a fight that matters.

Villains Are Essential for Heroes

Let me explain why conflict isn't just good for your brand. It's essential for your survival, using the most badass example of villain creation in business history.

Harley-Davidson doesn't just sell motorcycles. They sell rebellion against "The Man."

But here's what most people don't understand: Harley had to create "The Man" as their villain before they could position themselves as the hero fighting against it.

In the 1960s, Harley-Davidson was just another motorcycle company competing on features, price, and performance. Japanese bikes were faster, more reliable, and cheaper. By every rational measure, Harley should have been dead by 1970.

Instead, they created the most powerful villain in transportation history: conformity itself.

"The Man" became their catch-all enemy: corporate culture, suburban mediocrity, nine-to-five imprisonment, and the keeping-up-with-the-Joneses lifestyle. Suddenly, buying a Harley wasn't about transportation. It was about rejecting everything society expected you to be.

They turned motorcycle ownership into identity warfare.

Brands with clear enemies see 73% higher customer retention than those without. Harley's average customer lifetime value is $45,000, not because their bikes are objectively better, but because rebellion is priceless.

Every Honda became a symbol of practical thinking and boring choices. Every Yamaha represented efficiency over authenticity. Every Kawasaki stood for speed without soul. And every Harley? Every Harley was a middle finger to anyone who thought life should be safe, predictable, and sensible.

The genius wasn't the product. It was the enemy.

Harley customers didn't just buy motorcycles; they bought membership in a rebellion. They didn't just join a brand; they joined a war against conformity. They didn't just make a purchase; they made a statement about who they refused to become.

The result? **Harley customers literally tattoo the company logo on their bodies.** When's the last time you saw someone with a Honda tattoo?

Harley customers spend 4x more on brand merchandise than Honda customers because you don't accessorize transportation, you accessorize rebellion.

This is what happens when you give people something bigger than themselves to fight against.

But here's the beautiful part: "The Man" was the perfect villain because it was big enough to justify lifelong commitment. You can't defeat conformity with a single purchase. You have to keep fighting it every day, with every choice, including every motorcycle you buy.

Harley created a war that could never be won, which meant customers could never stop fighting.

Compare this to brands without villains. They compete on features, price, and incremental improvements. They fight for market share instead of fighting for meaning. Their customers compare specifications instead of joining movements.

Brands without enemies create transactions. Brands with enemies create transformations.

When someone buys a Harley, they're not just acquiring transportation; they're declaring independence from societal expectations. They're not just joining a brand community; they're enlisting in a lifelong rebellion.

That's not customer loyalty. That's customer devotion.

Here's the psychological principle at work: **Humans are tribal animals who define themselves as much by what they're against as by what they're for.** When you give people a common enemy, you give them a common identity. When you give them a common identity, you give them uncommon loyalty.

The strongest bonds are formed in opposition to something, not just in support of something.

Your brand needs an enemy because your customers need a cause. They need to feel like their choices matter for something bigger than product features. They need to believe that supporting your brand means fighting against something they genuinely despise.

Without a villain to fight against, your hero has nothing heroic to do.

And customers don't tattoo boring brands on their bodies.

The Tech Wars: Slack and Zoom as Villain Slayers

Look at Slack. Their villain wasn't Microsoft Outlook or Gmail; it was the endless purgatory of email itself. Slack declared war on inbox hell: long threads, wasted time, lost files. Their rallying cry? *"Email is where information goes to die."* Suddenly, Slack wasn't just a tool; it was an uprising against corporate inefficiency.

Or Zoom. Their enemy wasn't competitors like WebEx; it was commuting, wasted hours in traffic, and the soul-sucking grind of fluorescent conference rooms. Their story was simple: *"Time is life. Why waste it driving when you could click?"*

Neither brand sold software features. They sold escape routes from villains everyone already hated. And that's why millions joined their revolutions.

Right now, name your brand's biggest enemy. If you said "our competitors," you're thinking like an accountant, not a revolutionary. Competitors are just other companies. Enemies are systems worth destroying.

If your customers aren't enlisting in your war, you're not fighting the right enemy.

How to Manufacture Conflict

Now let me teach you the art of villain creation: how to identify enemies worth fighting and conflicts worth manufacturing without destroying your business in the process.

First rule: Your villain should be bigger than your competition.

Competitors fight for market share. Enemies fight for the soul of your industry. Guess which battle creates more passionate soldiers?

Don't make Nike your enemy if you're Adidas; make "settling for good enough" your enemy. Don't make McDonald's your villain if you're Burger King; make "fake food culture" your villain. Don't make Apple your enemy if you're Samsung; make "technological elitism" your villain.

Big villains create big heroes. Small villains create small wars.

Watch this principle in action with the most delicious villain creation in recent history: **Oatly versus Big Dairy.**

Oatly could have positioned itself as "another milk alternative." It could have competed on taste, nutrition, or price. It could have played it safe in the crowded plant-based beverage space.

Instead, it declared war on an entire industry.

Their villain wasn't other oat milk brands. It was the entire dairy industrial complex. Not specific companies, but the whole system of factory farming, environmental destruction, and animal exploitation that traditional milk represents.

"It's like milk, but made for humans," became their rallying cry. Oatly's slogan wasn't just cheeky copywriting; it was a declaration of war that made every dairy cow a casualty of environmental consciousness. Every ad was an attack on dairy industry assumptions. Every package design was a middle finger to milk marketing conventions.

They didn't just sell oat milk; they sold rebellion against Big Dairy. They didn't just offer an alternative; they offered a revolution.

The conflict was brilliant because it was ethical, strategic, and profitable.

Ethical because factory farming genuinely harms the environment and animals. Strategic because it positioned every dairy company as the villain. Profitable because it gave customers a moral reason to pay premium prices for plant milk.

But here's the genius move: They attacked the system, not the people.

Oatly never called milk drinkers stupid or evil. They never shamed individual consumers. They attacked the industry that sold milk, not the people who bought it. This gave milk drinkers permission to switch sides without admitting they'd been wrong.

The best villains are systems, not people. The best conflicts are about principles, not personalities.

The Archetype Advantage

Joseph Campbell's Hero's Journey wasn't just about myths. It's the blueprint for every blockbuster, every legend, every brand story that sticks. And at its core is always the same tension: hero versus villain.

- **The Call to Adventure:** Your customer realizes the old system (the villain) is failing them.
- **Crossing the Threshold:** They take the risk of trying your brand.
- **The Trials:** They face resistance, critics, habits, inertia, but you equip them with tools and courage.
- **The Transformation:** By choosing you, they don't just buy a product; they become someone new.
- **The Return:** They re-enter their world as a hero, aligned with a cause larger than themselves.

When your brand positions the villain clearly, you're not just selling; you're pulling your customers into a myth where they're the protagonist and you're their weapon.

Villain-Naming Drill

Grab a marker. On a single sheet of paper, write:

"Our brand exists to destroy _____."

Fill in the blank with one system, mindset, or cultural lie that makes your blood boil. Not a competitor, a villain. Something big enough that your customers will nod, clench their fists, and say, *"Hell yes, I hate that too."*

If you can't name your villain in one sentence, you don't have one.

Battle Plan: Declare Your War

1. **Name your villain.** Not a competitor. A system, mindset, or cultural lie that pisses you off enough to burn it down. Write it in all caps on your office wall. If it doesn't scare your PR team, it's too small.
2. **Define your battlefield.** Decide where this war will be fought: advertising, product design, packaging, events, social media. You need one primary arena where your enemy feels your fire.
3. **Crown your hero.** Craft your story so you (and your customers) are positioned as the obvious solution to the

villain you've named. Make it impossible to buy from you without joining the fight.

4. **Arm your tribe.** Create symbols, slogans, merchandise, hashtags, rituals. Anything that lets customers signal their allegiance. Wars are won with banners and chants as much as weapons.

5. **Announce the first strike.** Publish one bold, public declaration of war that makes your villain visible and forces people to take sides. Don't whisper it. Shout it.

6. **Track the battles.** Share every win against your villain, no matter how small. Momentum builds loyalty. Victories prove the war is real.

7. **Never surrender.** Once you pick your enemy, don't back down. Even when it costs you. Especially when it costs you. Cowards pivot. Heroes persist.

Do this now: Write a one-sentence declaration of war your brand could issue tomorrow. If it wouldn't make your competitors sweat, your mother gasp, and your customers cheer, rewrite it until it does.

Your Villain's Obituary

Write the obituary for the system or mindset your brand exists to kill.

Example:

"Here lies The Commute. For decades it stole hours, patience, and lives, forcing millions into traffic jams and fluorescent boardrooms. It died when technology proved that productivity doesn't require highways or cubicles. The world is freer, faster, and saner without it. Rest in pieces."

Now write yours. What dies when your brand wins? What will the world celebrate once your villain is gone? That obituary should make your customers cheer and your competitors sweat.

CHAPTER 7
Convert Like a Cult

Outrage + exclusivity + belonging

Let me tell you something that'll make your marketing team deeply uncomfortable: **Your customers don't want to buy from you; they want to worship you. And the brands that understand this psychological hunger don't just build businesses; they build religions that outlast empires.**

Not the Kool-Aid-drinking, compound-living, apocalypse-preparing kind of cults. I'm talking about the psychological mechanics that create unshakeable devotion, tribal identity, and behavior that looks completely irrational to outsiders.

Think I'm exaggerating? Let me ask you this:

When's the last time you saw someone camp outside a store for three days to buy a product? When's the last time you saw customers defend a brand so aggressively they'll attack friends who use competitors? When's the last time you saw people tattoo corporate logos on their bodies, wear brand uniforms when they're not at work, or build their entire identity around the products they consume?

That's not customer loyalty. That's cult behavior. And it's fucking brilliant.

Because here's what traditional marketing will never tell you: **Rational customers are the worst customers.** They compare prices. They switch brands for minor benefits. They view your product as a commodity to be optimized rather than an identity to be embraced.

Cult members don't comparison shop. They convert others. They defend the faith. They pay premium prices gladly because they're not buying products. They're buying belonging.

Your loyalty program offers points and discounts. Cults offer meaning and identity. Guess which one creates customers willing to die for the brand?

This chapter is about the dark psychology of conversion. How to create rituals that bond customers to your brand, exclusivity that makes people desperate to belong, and symbolism so powerful that rational people will permanently mark their bodies with your corporate imagery.

Warning: This is advanced-level brand building. Use these techniques responsibly, authentically, and only if

you're prepared for the kind of customer devotion that borders on religious fervor.

And yes, I can hear your legal team having conniptions about the word *cult*. Tell them customer obsession is only illegal if you're selling Kool-Aid. We're selling identity.

Time to build a congregation that worships at the altar of your brand.

Why Brands Need Rituals

Let me destroy a myth that's been killing businesses for decades: **the belief that customers make rational purchase decisions based on features, benefits, and price comparisons.**

This is corporate fantasy. The kind of delusion that leads to endless PowerPoints about "value propositions" while completely ignoring the psychological forces that actually drive human behavior.

Here's reality: Humans are ritual animals who crave meaning, repetition, and ceremonial belonging.

We don't just want products; we want practices. We don't just want purchases; we want participation. We don't just want features; we want rituals that reinforce our identity and connect us to our tribe.

The brands that understand this don't just sell products. They create religions.

Want proof? Let's talk about the greatest ritual machine in modern fitness: **CrossFit.**

CrossFit didn't just create workouts. They created an entire ritual system designed to turn exercise into religious ceremony. Every aspect of the experience is engineered to addict, to bond, and to convert.

- **The Ritual of Initiation:** You don't just "join" CrossFit. You're "on-ramped" through a special process that marks you as different from the average gym-goer. Initiation separates insiders from outsiders.
- **The Ritual of Language:** WODs. PRs. AMRAPs. EMOMs. A secret language that only believers understand. Learn it, and you belong.
- **The Ritual of Suffering:** Brutal workouts that push you to collapse. Shared pain creates stronger bonds than shared pleasure. Nothing cements tribe membership faster than sweating and suffering together.
- **The Ritual of Celebration:** Every rep counts. Every PR gets applause. The community celebrates individual victories like tribal triumphs.
- **The Ritual of Conversion:** CrossFitters can't shut the hell up. Every dinner, every office chat, every family reunion, they're evangelizing their "box," their WOD,

their progress. Recruitment isn't marketing; it's worship.

The result? CrossFit grew from zero to 15,000 gyms worldwide in 15 years. Members pay triple the average gym membership. They travel across states for competitions. They tattoo the fucking logo on their bodies.

Traditional gyms? They hand you a membership card, leave you to wander a sea of machines, and wonder why their churn rate is 60%.

Traditional gyms create customers. CrossFit creates disciples.

Your brand is either giving people rituals that reinforce their belonging, or you're giving them nothing but receipts.

Stop selling workouts. Stop selling software. Stop selling clothes. Start creating rituals that satisfy the deepest human craving: the craving to belong.

Ritual Design for the Rest of Us

You don't need Harley tattoos or Supreme mobs to create rituals. Even small brands can engineer ceremonies that feel sacred. Here's how:

1. **Identify existing habits.** What do customers already do when they use your product? Drinking coffee, unboxing, logging in? Start there.

2. **Add a ceremonial twist.** Can you formalize the moment? A hashtag, a phrase, a repeatable action? Rituals are just habits with meaning attached.

3. **Create shared language.** Give your tribe words outsiders don't use. It builds belonging through vocabulary.

4. **Mark milestones.** Celebrate the 10th purchase, the first year, the first referral. Ritualize achievements.

5. **Encourage evangelism.** Design small actions customers can use to "convert" others: stickers, starter packs, referral stories.

Rituals don't need scale. They need consistency. Build them small, repeat them often, and watch them grow into ceremonies.

Exclusivity and Belonging

Now for the paradox that terrifies most executives: **The more exclusive you make your brand, the more desperately people want to belong to it.**

Business school teaches the opposite: maximize reach, broaden access, lower barriers. Inclusivity equals growth, right? Wrong. **Exclusivity equals devotion.**

Because humans don't crave what everyone can have. We crave what's scarce, hard to get, and dripping with status.

Nobody's camping out for the McRib. But people will sleep on concrete for an iPhone launch. Why? Because one signals exclusivity and cultural significance, and the other signals limited-time fast food diarrhea.

The supreme example, literally, is Supreme.

Supreme turned shopping into a blood sport. Every Thursday at 11 AM EST, they drop a limited collection. Not pre-orders. Not infinite stock. A finite number of items that vanish in seconds.

The result? Customers camp outside stores for days. They set up bot networks online. They coordinate like military units to secure hoodies. The resale market flips items for 3–10x retail within hours.

Supreme could manufacture more. They choose not to. Scarcity is their profit center. Exclusivity is their engine.

Supreme creates three groups every drop:

- **The Chosen Few:** Those who score. They become walking gods of insider status.
- **The Rejected Many:** Those who fail. Instead of giving up, they double down. They get hungrier. They fight harder next time.

- **The Observers:** Even those who don't buy watch with fascination. They spread the story. They reinforce the myth.

That's not commerce. It's conversion.

Even in B2B, this works. Salesforce doesn't just sell CRM; they sell Trailblazer identity. Badges, certifications, annual Dreamforce pilgrimages. It's religion disguised as enterprise software.

Exclusivity isn't about shutting people out. It's about making entry feel like achievement.

Your brand doesn't need to be accessible to everyone. It needs to be irresistible to someone.

Why Rituals Feel Holy

Anthropologists know what CMOs ignore: ritual is humanity's oldest software.

From tribal initiations to Sunday sermons, rituals serve three universal functions:

- **Identity.** "You are now one of us."
- **Continuity.** "This is who we've always been."
- **Transcendence.** "You are part of something bigger."

Brands tap the same wiring. A CrossFit WOD feels like a tribal hunt. A Supreme drop feels like a pilgrimage. A Harley ride feels like a sacred procession.

It's not manipulation; it's anthropology. Humans crave ritual because rituals make life feel less random. They transform consumption into meaning. And meaning is what keeps people coming back.

How to Create Tattoo-Worthy Brands

Here's the ultimate loyalty test: **Would your customers tattoo your logo on their body?**

Sounds insane? Tell that to Harley-Davidson, which has more tattoos than some religions. Nearly half of Harley riders have ink. You ever seen someone ink the Toyota logo on their chest? Didn't think so.

Harley tattoos aren't about motorcycles. They're about freedom, rebellion, authenticity. They're about declaring allegiance to a tribe and a way of life.

Tattoo-worthy brands share five traits:

1. **Values bigger than products.** Harley sells freedom. Apple sells creativity. Nike sells transcendence.
2. **Tribal belonging.** Tattoos aren't fashion; they're identity markers.
3. **Transformation stories.** Tattoos commemorate meaningful life shifts.
4. **Symbolic power.** The logo itself matters. Distinctive, bold, loaded with meaning.

5. **Ritual significance.** Tattoos often follow transformative brand experiences: first ride, first race, first WOD.

If your logo doesn't represent values, community, and transformation, it won't earn skin space.

But if your brand changes lives, you can expect to see your symbol etched into flesh.

That's not loyalty. That's immortality.

Cult Brand Red Flags

Here's the danger no one admits: cults can turn toxic. And brands that confuse devotion with domination don't end up legendary. They end up infamous.

Watch for these red flags:

- **Obsession without reciprocity.** When customers give everything but the brand gives nothing back. That's exploitation, not loyalty.
- **Blind conformity.** When customers stop thinking for themselves and parrot slogans without question. Healthy devotion still leaves room for individuality.
- **Hostility toward outsiders.** When your tribe spends more time attacking the competition than celebrating your mission, your cult has turned cannibal.

- **Leadership idolatry.** When the founder becomes the deity instead of the values. One scandal and the whole religion crumbles.

True cult brands channel intensity into identity, not toxicity. You don't want zombies. You want zealots who think, act, and spread your message with pride.

Welcome to the Congregation

You now know the secret: **Rituals bind. Exclusivity converts. Symbols immortalize.**

CrossFit turned workouts into ceremonies. Supreme turned shopping into war. Harley turned motorcycles into eternal identity.

These aren't accidents. They're deliberate architectures of belief.

Your brand can do the same, but only if you stop chasing customers and start creating converts. Stop writing "mission statements" and start writing scriptures. Stop offering discounts and start offering devotion.

Because here's the brutal truth: Your competitors are optimizing funnels. You could be building temples. They're chasing transactions. You could be building religions.

The marketplace doesn't need more vendors. It needs prophets.

Your congregation is waiting.

Your Ritual Drill

List three rituals your customers already practice when using your product. Maybe it's the way they unbox it, share it online, or talk about it with friends.

Now ask: how can you formalize those rituals into repeatable brand ceremonies?

- Can you name the moment?
- Can you give them a symbol, a phrase, a celebration?
- Can you invite them to share the ritual with others?

Your job isn't to invent rituals from scratch. It's to notice the ones already happening and elevate them into sacred ceremonies your customers will repeat for life.

CHAPTER 8
Comedy as a Conversion Tool

If you can't make them laugh, they won't buy

Here's a truth that'll make brand managers break into a cold sweat: **While your competitors are boring people to death with "professional messaging," you could be making audiences laugh so hard they throw money at you. But you're too chickenshit to try.**

While they're agonizing over "polite" copy that offends nobody but excites nobody, while they're A/B testing lifeless headlines that generate 0.3% click-through rates, while they're spending millions on "brand awareness" campaigns that make no one aware of anything except their own mediocrity. You could be hijacking attention, stealing the spotlight, and cementing loyalty with the oldest psychological hack in human history: laughter.

Because here's the thing every comedian knows and every corporate drone ignores: Laughter is involuntary agreement.

When someone laughs at your content, you're not just entertaining them; you're hacking their neurology. Their body floods with dopamine, endorphins, and oxytocin. Their brain decides, unconsciously and instantly: *"I like these people. I trust these people. I want to be around these people."*

That's not "engagement." That's biochemical bonding.

And the kicker? **Comedy doesn't just get attention; it gets permission.** Permission to bypass logical defenses. Permission to sneak ideas past people's skepticism. Permission to lodge your worldview so deep in their psyche that they'll defend it like their own.

So why don't more brands use it? Simple: they're cowards. Comedy requires personality. It requires risks. It requires being okay with some people not getting it. It requires confidence. And most brands would rather be blandly safe than dangerously unforgettable.

But here's the brutal truth: Safe brands don't scale. Funny brands dominate.

This chapter is about how to use humor not as a gimmick but as a conversion machine. We'll break down the psychology of laughter, the mechanics of comedic branding, and the tactical playbook that takes you from "professional" to "unignorable."

Why Comedy Disarms Faster Than Discounts

Marketers love to believe people buy rationally: price comparisons, feature evaluations, bullet-point value props. That's bullshit.

Here's neurological reality: Emotions drive decisions. Logic comes after to justify them.

When you laugh, your brain is literally rewarding you. The limbic system processes emotions five times faster than the neocortex processes logic. Which means if you make someone laugh, you've already won before their rational brain even shows up.

Think about it: when was the last time you remembered a feature list? Now think about the last time you remembered a joke. Which one stuck? Which one did you repeat? Which one made you feel something?

That's why comedy annihilates boring competitors. It bypasses resistance and implants memory.

Look at **Old Spice.** By 2010, they were a relic, your grandfather's deodorant. They could've gone the rational route: new formulations, clinical comparisons, boring product charts. Instead, they dropped *The Man Your Man Could Smell Like.*

Isaiah Mustafa, shirtless, absurd, rapid-fire lines delivered with hypnotic confidence:

> "Hello ladies. Look at your man, now back to me, now back at your man, now back to me. Sadly, he isn't me..."

The ad didn't explain features. It didn't talk about ingredients. It made people laugh. And that laugh created instant emotional permission.

The result? A 125% sales increase in six months. 75% market share. A corpse brand resurrected into cultural relevance.

Why? Because humor sells where logic fails.

Discounts appeal to greed. Comedy appeals to joy. And joy beats greed every damn time.

When Humor Backfires

Of course, not all brand comedy lands. When humor misfires, it's not just unfunny; it's catastrophic.

Pepsi's Kendall Jenner protest ad tried to turn social justice into a punchline. It wasn't satire; it was cringe. Instead of connecting, it trivialized real movements, reducing outrage and struggle to a soda commercial. The backlash was instant, global, and brutal. Pepsi wasn't funny; they were tone-deaf.

Same with brands that thought COVID was "a great chance for pandemic jokes." Twitter roasted them alive. When people are scared for their lives, "quirky" humor about hand sanitizer shortages doesn't make you clever; it makes you callous.

The lesson? Comedy must punch up, not down. It must expose truth, not exploit trauma. Make fun of power, hypocrisy, or your own industry bullshit, not people in pain.

Punchlines > Taglines

Here's the death sentence for 99% of brands: **They mistake taglines for personality.**

Taglines explain. Punchlines convert. Taglines are safe, polished, corporate. Punchlines are sharp, memorable, contagious.

Nobody quotes a tagline at a party. But they'll repeat a punchline until it becomes part of pop culture.

Enter **Dollar Shave Club.**

They could've launched with a boring tagline: *"Affordable razors delivered."* Instead, they blew up the shaving industry with comedy.

"Hi, I'm Mike. Our blades are f***ing great."
That's not a tagline. That's a punchline that became a meme.

Every joke in their launch video doubled as positioning:

- "Do you like spending $20 a month on brand-name razors? Nineteen goes to Roger Federer." → Razor prices are a scam.
- "I'm not a razor. I'm your dad's razor." → We're authentic, not over-marketed.

Result? A $4,500 video → 26 million views, 12,000 customers in 48 hours, $1 billion exit to Unilever.

The lesson: Taglines are forgotten. Punchlines are shared.

Stop "informing" people. Start entertaining them. Start creating lines they'll quote in bars, texts, and TikToks.

Roast Your Industry, Toast Your Brand

Now let's get dangerous. The highest form of comedic branding isn't just telling jokes; it's roasting your industry while positioning yourself as the rebel alternative.

This is comedic warfare. It's calling out the bullshit everyone sees but no one says. It's naming the elephant in the boardroom and turning it into your mascot.

Done wrong, you look like a petty jerk. Done right, you look like a prophet.

Look at **Ryan Reynolds with Aviation Gin.**

The alcohol industry is stuffed with fake sophistication, pretentious ads, and celebrity endorsements that nobody believes. Reynolds torched it all while selling his own gin.

- "Aviation Gin. Owned by a Canadian." → Honest, self-aware, funny.
- "I own Aviation Gin. That's a real thing that happened." → Mocking endorsement culture while actually endorsing.
- "We're probably not for everyone. Actually, we're definitely not for everyone." → Exclusive honesty wrapped in humor.

Every ad was both a roast of industry bullshit and a toast to Aviation Gin's authenticity. Result? A $610 million acquisition.

The formula: Roast systems, not people. Include yourself in the joke. Offer better alternatives.

When you mock your industry's absurdities with wit, you don't just get laughs; you get authority. You become the truth-teller, the brand with balls, the only one willing to say what everyone's thinking.

The Four Archetypes of Brand Comedy

All great brand humor falls into a few archetypes. Pick one and commit:

- **Satire:** Mocking industry absurdities with sharp wit. (Aviation Gin roasting celebrity endorsements.)
- **Parody:** Imitating a known format, then twisting it. (Old Spice spoofing the "serious" cologne ad.)
- **Absurdism:** Embracing the surreal to stand out. (Mailchimp's "Did you mean MailShrimp?" campaign.)
- **Dark Comedy:** Tackling uncomfortable truths with brutal honesty. (Cards Against Humanity's "holiday hole" campaign where people paid to literally dig a hole.)

The danger? Mixing all of them until you sound like a try-hard improv troupe. Choose your archetype, sharpen it, and own it.

How to Write Jokes That Sell

Let's get tactical. Comedy isn't magic. It's structure. Here's your 5-step framework:

1. **Setup the truth.** Start with something customers already know. Example: Razors are overpriced.
2. **Spot the absurdity.** Find the ridiculous angle. Example: You're paying Roger Federer's salary.

3. **Exaggerate for effect.** Push it further. Example: "Do you like spending $20 a month on brand-name razors? Nineteen goes to Roger Federer."
4. **Flip expectations.** Take the logical path, then twist. Example: "I'm not a razor. I'm your dad's razor."
5. **Anchor to benefits.** Tie the laugh back to your value. Example: "Our blades are f***ing great."

If you can make people laugh **and** understand why your product matters in the same sentence, you've won.

The Comedy Stress Test

Before you unleash your brand joke on the world, run it through this checklist:

1. **Would my audience laugh, or would my legal team panic?** (Hint: if it's the latter, you might be onto something.)
2. **Does it punch up, not down?** Always target systems, clichés, and power, not your customers.
3. **Does it tie back to my brand's truth?** If the laugh doesn't connect to your value, it's just noise.
4. **Would I share this with a friend?** If it's not screenshot-worthy, it's not ready.
5. **Will some people hate it?** If the answer is no, it's probably too safe to matter.

Comedy isn't just about laughs; it's about creating the right kind of tension, then paying it off with truth.

The Last Laugh

Here's the brutal truth: **Your competitors are explaining features while you could be creating fans.**

Old Spice didn't change their deodorant. They changed their personality. Dollar Shave Club didn't reinvent razors. They reinvented razor marketing. Ryan Reynolds didn't rewrite alcohol. He rewrote alcohol advertising.

The funny brands don't just sell; they seduce. They don't just inform; they infect culture. They don't just compete; they conquer.

The world is drowning in boring brand noise. Nobody remembers your tagline. Nobody gives a shit about your spec sheet. But everyone remembers the joke that made them spit out coffee at work. Everyone shares the ad that made them laugh so hard they had to show it to friends. Everyone feels warmer toward the brand that actually made their day better.

Comedy is the only marketing strategy that makes customers grateful for your ads.

So the choice is yours: keep writing serious content that nobody cares about, or start writing funny content that people love enough to spread for free.

Your competitors are still terrified of risk. That's your opening. That's your edge. That's your revolution.

Stop selling to customers. Start entertaining them. Stop aiming for respect. Start aiming for laughter. Because the brand that makes them laugh hardest is the brand they'll buy fastest.

The Comedy Playbook: How to Weaponize Humor for Conversion

You've laughed. You've nodded. You've maybe even squirmed a little. But now it's time to do the work. This isn't just theory; it's battle instructions. Here's how to actually make comedy your conversion weapon.

Step 1: Choose Your Comic Persona

Your brand needs a comedic voice, not just random jokes. Decide:

- Are you the **Deadpan Assassin** (Aviation Gin)?
- The **Loud Absurdist** (Old Spice)?
- The **Self-Aware Underdog** (Dollar Shave Club)?
- The **Quirky Oddball** (Mailchimp)?

This persona becomes your brand's stand-up act. Without consistency, you're just flailing.

Step 2: Identify the Industry Bullshit

Comedy feeds on truth. List all the clichés, lies, and hypocrisies your industry depends on. Those are your setups. Every "premium" claim, every fake lifestyle ad, every polished piece of corporate cringe is material waiting to be roasted.

Step 3: Write Punchlines, Not Taglines

Take your core value proposition and exaggerate it until it's funny. Example:

- Boring: "We deliver razors affordably."
- Punchline: "Our blades are f***ing great, and they cost less than a latte."

  If your line couldn't make someone smirk in a bar, it won't make them share it online.

Step 4: Turn Ads into Entertainment

Stop writing ads. Start writing sketches, roasts, memes, and bits. Old Spice wasn't an ad; it was a mini comedy routine. Ryan Reynolds' Aviation spots weren't ads; they were parodies. If your campaign wouldn't make sense as a Netflix short, it's too boring.

Step 5: Make Fun of Yourself First

Self-deprecation disarms cynicism. Nobody likes brands that only punch outward. Admit your flaws, laugh at your quirks, roast your own conventions. Customers will trust you more because you're not pretending to be perfect.

Step 6: Bake Comedy into Every Touchpoint

- **Website copy:** Kill the jargon. Replace it with wit.
- **Product packaging:** Make the unboxing itself a laugh. (See: Cards Against Humanity.)
- **Emails:** Stop writing like a robot. Add one unexpected joke to the subject line.
- **Customer service:** Give reps permission to be funny humans, not corporate drones.

  If you're funny in ads but boring everywhere else, it feels fake. Comedy must be systemic.

Step 7: Crowdsource Your Funny

Your funniest stuff might come from your fans. Meme culture is brand rocket fuel. Encourage customers to make parodies, remixes, and jokes. Share them. Celebrate them. Make your community co-writers of the act.

Step 8: Test Like a Comedian, Not a Marketer

Comedians test material in small clubs before Netflix specials. You should test your jokes in social posts before million-dollar campaigns. What gets the most shares, likes, and laughs? That's your killer bit.

Step 9: Tie Every Laugh to a Sale

Never forget: humor is a vehicle, not the destination. Every joke must connect back to why your product matters. Otherwise, you're just a clown juggling for free while your competitors close the deal.

Step 10: Keep Pushing Boundaries

Safe jokes die. Risky jokes spread. Comedy is about tension and release. The tension is risk; the release is laughter. If your legal team loves your script, your audience won't.

Your Battle Orders

1. Audit your last 10 pieces of content. Highlight every sentence that could appear in a tax form. Kill it. Replace it with something a human would say.
2. Write three "roast lines" about your industry's biggest absurdities. Pick the sharpest one and turn it into your next ad headline.
3. Run one campaign this quarter where your only goal is to make your audience laugh, then measure the conversion lift compared to your serious content.
4. Empower one brave employee to tweet like a stand-up comic for 30 days. Track what happens.

5. Create one piece of packaging, onboarding copy, or customer email so funny that people take screenshots and post it online.

Bottom line: Safe brands die. Funny brands live forever.

Your competitors are still whispering features while you could be shouting punchlines. They're still explaining. You're going to entertain. They're still begging for attention. You're going to be the thing customers *crave* to see.

The last laugh belongs to the brand brave enough to risk it. Make sure that's you.

Your Punchline Drill

Write three punchlines that roast your industry's clichés while spotlighting your strengths. Here are examples:

1. *"Our competitors brag about being 'innovative.' Cute. So is a toaster."*
2. *"Everyone says they 'put the customer first.' We actually put you second, right after common sense."*
3. *"The industry calls this a 'feature.' We call it what it is: an excuse to charge you more."*

A good punchline makes your audience laugh, nod, and trust you in the same breath. If it stings your industry, even better.

CHAPTER 9

The Fan Factory

Turn strangers into evangelists

Here's the marketing truth that'll make your customer acquisition team question their entire existence: **Your ad budget is bloated, your funnels are fragile, and your spreadsheets are lying to you. The only marketing engine that scales without limits is the one you don't control: your fans.**

While you're dropping six figures a month on paid ads, buying attention like an addict chasing their next dopamine hit, your best customers are out there doing your job better than you. For free. They're recommending you in DMs. They're defending you in comment wars. They're turning dinner parties into sales pitches and Slack threads into recruitment campaigns.

And here's the brutal math: **One passionate fan influences more people in a year than your best ad will in a decade.** Nielsen calls it "word of mouth." Psychologists call it "social proof." I call it the **Fan Factory**, the systematic process of turning buyers into believers, believers into disciples, and disciples into evangelists who treat your success like their personal mission.

But let's draw the line in blood right now: **Customer satisfaction isn't enough.** A satisfied customer buys again. A fan convinces five other people to buy for the first time. A satisfied customer shrugs when someone bad-mouths you. A fan draws their sword and defends you like family.

If you can't name three customers who would fight trolls on your behalf, you don't have fans; you have receipts.

This chapter is about manufacturing devotion. It's about building an army of unpaid apostles who out-recruit your sales team, out-market your ad agency, and outlast every quarter's churn cycle. **Because the difference between a customer and a fan is the difference between a transaction and a transformation.**

The Fan Journey Framework

Let's torch the biggest lie in CRM: that "all customers should be treated the same." That's like saying all strangers on Tinder deserve marriage proposals.

Here's the real spectrum:

- **Stage 1: Strangers** – They don't know you exist.
- **Stage 2: Lurkers** – They're watching but not engaging.

- **Stage 3: Fans** – They're liking, sharing, and smiling at your memes.
- **Stage 4: Disciples** – They're converting others. They've become recruiters.
- **Stage 5: Evangelists** – They've merged their identity with your brand.

Most companies drown in the middle, endlessly entertaining lurkers while never weaponizing fans.

Take **Apple** as the masterclass:

- Strangers saw the first iPhone and became lurkers because it was too damn intriguing to ignore.
- Lurkers became fans by walking into Apple Stores that felt more like temples than retail spaces.
- Fans became disciples when owning an iPhone wasn't just a purchase but a values statement: design > conformity.
- Disciples became evangelists when product launches became holy days, and unboxings became ceremonies.
- Evangelists became unpaid employees, defending Apple on Reddit, creating how-to blogs, and tattooing the logo on their bodies.

Every stage adds exponential value:

- Strangers = attention
- Lurkers = eyeballs
- Fans = engagement

- Disciples = conversions
- Evangelists = multiplication

And here's the crucial law: **You can't skip stages.** You can't drag a stranger into evangelism with one clever ad. You have to guide them through each transformation, deliberately, systematically, ruthlessly.

Case Study: K-pop, the Fan Factory on Steroids

If you want to see the Fan Journey in its purest, most weaponized form, look at K-pop fandoms. BTS doesn't just have fans; they have ARMY, an army in the literal sense. Strangers stumble across a music video → lurkers binge the content → fans buy albums in triplicate → disciples organize streaming parties → evangelists crash Twitter trending topics and flood global charity campaigns in their idols' names.

K-pop companies design the fan journey like a military campaign. They weaponize inside language, coded emojis, fan chants, synchronized light sticks, and exclusive online communities. The result? Fans don't just consume music; they feel like soldiers in a cultural movement.

The lesson: devotion isn't an accident. It's engineered with rituals, symbols, and stages. K-pop didn't just build bands; they built fan factories.

How to Engineer Virality

Brands love to say, "virality can't be planned." That's corporate cowardice. Virality is an equation: **Social Currency + Emotion + Participation + Scarcity + Urgency = Spread.**

Look at the **ALS Ice Bucket Challenge**.

- Social currency: You looked brave, charitable, and connected.
- Emotion: Shock, joy, moral superiority all at once.
- Participation: Pour water, film it, nominate friends.
- Scarcity: You had 24 hours to do it.
- Multiplication: Each person tagged three more.

Result? $115 million raised. 17 million videos. Global domination.

Virality wasn't an accident. It was a factory. Every part of the design made sharing feel better than not sharing. That's the playbook:

- **Give them status** – Sharing must make people look smart, funny, or virtuous.
- **Stack emotions** – Mix surprise, delight, anger, and hope. One note doesn't make a song.
- **Make it public** – Private doesn't spread. Public is proof.
- **Lower the bar** – Participation must be idiot-proof.

- **Force multiplication** – Build in tagging, challenges, nominations.
- **Add urgency** – Deadlines drive momentum.

The golden rule: **People don't share to help you. They share to upgrade their own identity.** Engineer for *that*, and virality becomes repeatable.

When Fans Do Your Job Better Than You

The holy grail isn't repeat buyers; it's fans who start running parts of your brand for you.

LEGO Ideas is the blueprint. Instead of just designing sets internally, LEGO gave fans a platform to pitch and vote. Designs that passed 10,000 votes got made and credited to the fan.

Fans didn't just participate; they out-innovated the company. NASA Women of NASA? Outsold official sets. Ship in a Bottle? Instant cult hit. Birds? Spawned a whole product line.

Here's why it worked:
- Fans got recognition, royalties, and bragging rights.
- LEGO got constant innovation and free marketing.
- The community got meaning.

The fans weren't buying LEGO. They were *building* LEGO.

Tesla does this with user-made promo videos that outperform their in-house ads. Slack does it with community tutorials that onboard new users better than official docs. CrossFit does it with WODs created by members.

The brutal truth: If your fans aren't out-creating your team, you've either starved them of tools or made them too bored to care.

When Fans Turn Against You

Here's the shadow side of fandom: the more power you give fans, the more dangerous they become if they feel betrayed.

Look at how quickly once-devoted communities can flip. Video game developers who delay launches? Their biggest evangelists become the loudest haters, flooding forums with rage. Musicians who "sell out"? Their disciples torch them online for abandoning the cause. Even K-pop fandoms, so disciplined in their loyalty, have mutinied when they feel disrespected or ignored.

When fans hijack the narrative, they don't just complain; they mobilize. They meme, they trend, they drag. And because their devotion was once your greatest weapon, their betrayal hits like a nuclear strike.

The solution? Radical transparency. Admit mistakes fast. Keep the tribe looped in. Treat fans like stakeholders, not serfs. If they feel ownership, they'll forgive. If they feel discarded, they'll burn the temple down.

The Factory Floor

Here's the endgame: **Your job isn't to sell products. Your job is to manufacture evangelists.**

Because here's what separates good brands from immortal ones:

- Good brands buy attention. Great brands earn devotion.
- Good brands talk about themselves. Great brands let fans talk louder.
- Good brands build marketing departments. Great brands build movements.

But none of this works without authenticity. Fans can smell fake faster than your CFO can smell revenue decline. Manipulative communities implode. Synthetic virality backfires. Fake advocacy gets dragged in the comments section until you're a meme for all the wrong reasons.

The Fan Factory only runs on real fuel: **real value, real connection, real belonging.**

Your fans get meaning, identity, and status. You get growth without acquisition costs. They fight for you because they've fused with you. They create for you because creating makes them more themselves.

That's the trade. That's the factory.

So here's your choice:

- Keep renting customers with ads and watch your CAC climb into orbit.
- Or start manufacturing fans who build your empire for you—louder, faster, and cheaper than you ever could.

The factory is humming. The assembly line is waiting. Strangers are already sliding onto the conveyor belt.

Your competitors are still buying clicks. You're about to mint apostles.

Stop advertising. Start evangelizing. Stop running a business. Start running a religion.

The Fan Factory is open. What are you producing?

Fan Factory Playbook: How to Manufacture Evangelists

Step 1: Define Your Assembly Line

- Write down the five stages: Strangers → Lurkers → Fans → Disciples → Evangelists.

- Audit your funnel. Where are you strong? Where are you bleeding? Most brands are drowning in lurkers because they never give them a reason to cross the line.
- Stop wasting time trying to convert strangers with generic ads. Focus on moving people one stage at a time. That's the factory belt.

Worksheet: The Fan Conveyor Belt

Write down three names (real customers, not imaginary avatars). Place each at the stage they're currently in:

- Strangers
- Lurkers
- Fans
- Disciples
- Evangelists

Now answer: what specific action could move them one stage closer? A personalized DM? A VIP invite? A piece of content they can weaponize in arguments?

Your job isn't to teleport strangers into evangelists. It's to build the conveyor belt that moves them one stage at a time. If you can't map it, you can't manufacture it.

Step 2: Weaponize Social Currency

Ask this brutal question: *Does sharing us make someone look smarter, cooler, or more virtuous?*

If the answer is "meh," you're dead. Nobody risks their reputation to share mediocrity.

Redesign your content so it upgrades the identity of the sharer. If people don't gain status by spreading your message, your virality ceiling is zero.

Step 3: Engineer Rituals and Inside Language

Fans need ceremonies. Give them hashtags, memes, catchphrases, and rituals that outsiders won't understand.

Apple had "Think Different." CrossFit has WODs. Tesla has "Plaid mode." Your inside language = your gatekeeping tool.

Test: Could two fans meet at a bar, speak your language, and instantly bond as insiders? If not, build that language yesterday.

Step 4: Create Scarcity + Exclusivity

Fans don't brag about buying something everyone can buy. They brag about access.

Drop products, not catalogs. Launch events, not press releases. Build scarcity into your DNA.

Remember: **Exclusion creates desire; inclusion creates indifference.**

Step 5: Feed the Disciples with Ammunition

Disciples want to fight on your behalf, so arm them.

Create content they can screenshot, stats they can quote, memes they can weaponize.

Every argument about your brand should be winnable with the material you hand them.

Step 6: Let Evangelists Take the Stage

Stop hogging the mic. Showcase fan stories, fan creations, fan wins.

Give them spotlights that make them feel like legends inside your ecosystem. Recognition is oxygen for evangelists.

Brutal truth: Your community doesn't care about your CEO; they care about people like them who've been crowned heroes.

Step 7: Build Viral Mechanics into Everything

Don't wait for luck. Force multiplication into your system:

- o   Add nomination challenges.
- o   Add "tag three friends" CTAs.
- o   Add gamified milestones that demand sharing.

Every action should trigger three more. Fans should feel like recruiters, not just consumers.

Step 8: Hand Over the Tools

Fans should be creating content better than your team. Give them templates, platforms, remix rights.

Build a creator kit. Build a community hub. Build incentives that reward creativity.

Remember LEGO Ideas: your customers might design your next best product if you let them.

Step 9: Reward with Status, Not Just Discounts

Discounts breed bargain hunters. Status breeds evangelists.

Give badges, early access, limited editions, and insider privileges.

Your goal: make fans feel like they're part of the inner circle, not part of a loyalty program.

Step 10: Measure Devotion, Not Just Revenue

Stop obsessing over quarterly CAC and LTV. Track fan behaviors:

- o How many people are creating UGC without being paid?
- o How many people defend you in public?
- o How many referrals per customer are happening organically?

If these numbers aren't climbing, you don't have a fan factory; you have a cash register.

Brutal Directive

Your job isn't to "delight customers." Your job is to **forge evangelists who would rather die than see your brand dragged.**

Every campaign, every product, every community decision should answer one question: *Does this push someone one stage further down the factory line?*

If the answer is no, burn it.

Because your competitors are still burning money on Facebook ads while you could be minting apostles at scale.

Stop renting attention. Start manufacturing devotion. The Fan Factory never sleeps. Why the hell should you?

Your Fan Mapping Drill

Map three real customers across the Fan Journey stages:

1. **Customer A (Lurker):** They follow you but never engage. What's the nudge that would make them comment, share, or buy once?
2. **Customer B (Fan):** They like and share occasionally. What's the move that would make them recruit someone else?

3. **Customer C (Disciple):** They're already converting others. What reward, recognition, or ritual would transform them into an evangelist?

Devotion isn't magic; it's management. Move people stage by stage, and your customer list becomes a congregation.

CHAPTER 10

Playing for Legacy, Not Likes

Fame fades; legends endure

Here's the final truth that separates brands that matter from brands that disappear: **Every brand dies twice: first when it stops mattering, then when it stops existing. Most brands die the first death while still posting quarterly profits. You're about to learn how to achieve immortality instead.**

Legacies are measured in cultural permanence. In ideas that outlast their creators. In influence that compounds across generations. In the kind of impact that makes people say, decades later, "The world was different because this brand existed."

Your competitors are optimizing conversion funnels while you could be building cultural monuments. They're A/B testing headlines while you could be writing history.

But here's what makes most entrepreneurs and executives completely insane: Building for legacy

requires sacrificing short-term validation for long-term transformation.

It means choosing principles over profits when the two conflict. It means making decisions that might hurt this quarter's numbers but strengthen next decade's reputation. It means caring more about what your brand stands for than what your brand sells.

Most brands are playing for applause. Legendary brands play for history.

The applause seekers optimize for engagement metrics, viral content, and quarterly growth. They chase trending topics, pivot with market sentiment, and adjust their values based on focus group feedback. They build brands designed to be liked by everyone and remembered by no one.

The legacy builders do the opposite.

They ignore short-term noise to focus on long-term signal. They sacrifice breadth of appeal for depth of impact. They build brands so rooted in authentic purpose that they become cultural forces that shape society rather than just reflecting it.

This is your final choice: Do you want to be famous or do you want to be immortal?

Fame is temporary. Immortality is permanent. Fame depends on others' attention. Immortality creates others' inspiration. Fame makes you known. Immortality makes you necessary.

This chapter is about building brands that outlast trends, transcend industries, and create the kind of legacy that makes your company name synonymous with the change you brought to the world.

By the end, you'll understand why Steve Jobs obsessed over making "a dent in the universe," why Disney became cultural architecture rather than just entertainment, and how to build a brand legacy statement that transforms every business decision from tactical to transformational.

Warning: Legacy building requires courage most brands don't possess. The courage to stand for something bigger than profit and the patience to measure success in decades rather than quarters.

Time to build something immortal.

Why Likes Are Cheap, Loyalty Priceless

Let me start this final lesson by destroying the most dangerous delusion in modern marketing: **The belief that social media engagement metrics indicate brand health, customer loyalty, or business sustainability**.

This is not just wrong; it's actively destructive. The kind of thinking that leads brands to optimize for viral moments while their actual customer relationships deteriorate. The kind of strategy that creates millions of followers and zero advocates.

Here's the brutal reality: Likes are digital dopamine. Loyalty is economic permanence.

The average viral video is forgotten in 7 days. The average Disney movie is remembered for 70 years. TikTok influencers average 18 months of relevance. Legacy brands average 180 years of cultural impact.

Likes cost nothing to give and mean nothing to receive. They're the participation trophies of the attention economy, easy to earn, easier to forget, and completely disconnected from actual human behavior or business value.

Loyalty, on the other hand, is scarce, valuable, and irreplaceable.

Loyal customers pay premium prices during recessions. Loyal customers defend you during crises. Loyal customers recruit friends, family, and colleagues into your brand community. Loyal customers stick with you through product failures, service problems, and competitive pressure.

Likes disappear with algorithm changes. Loyalty survives market crashes.

Let me show you this principle in action by comparing two approaches to brand building: **the viral fame strategy versus the legacy loyalty strategy.**

Viral Fame Strategy: Optimize for short-term attention

Create content designed to trend. Chase viral moments. Pivot messaging based on social media feedback. Measure success through engagement metrics. Build audience through entertainment rather than value.

Result: Temporary relevance that disappears when the next trend emerges. Large but shallow audience that engages but doesn't purchase. Brand identity that shifts with cultural momentum rather than driving cultural change.

Legacy Loyalty Strategy: Optimize for long-term transformation

Create content designed to compound. Build consistent messaging. Develop principles that guide decisions regardless of external pressure. Measure success through customer lifetime value and cultural impact. Build audience through authentic value creation.

Result: Permanent relevance that strengthens over time. Smaller but deeper audience that purchases and advocates. Brand identity that shapes cultural momentum rather than following it.

The difference isn't just strategic; it's philosophical.

Viral fame brands treat customers as content consumers. Legacy loyalty brands treat customers as community members. Viral fame brands optimize for attention. Legacy loyalty brands optimize for transformation. Viral fame brands measure engagement. Legacy loyalty brands measure impact.

Want to see this distinction in its purest form? Compare TikTok influencers to Patagonia.

TikTok influencers generate millions of views, thousands of comments, and massive engagement rates. They're famous, talked about, and culturally relevant. TikTok influencers fight for attention spans. Patagonia fights for the planet. Guess which battle creates more loyal soldiers? **They're also completely replaceable.**

When their content stops trending, their audience moves to the next viral creator. When their platform changes, their influence disappears. When controversy emerges, their brand dies overnight.

Patagonia generates smaller audiences, fewer viral moments, and lower engagement rates. They're also completely irreplaceable.

Ninety-four percent of Fortune 500 companies from 1955 no longer exist, but brands like Coca-Cola (139 years) and Disney (100 years) keep getting stronger.

When environmental crises emerge, people look to Patagonia for leadership. When outdoor gear is needed, Patagonia is the trusted choice. When values-based consumers make purchase decisions, Patagonia represents authenticity in a world of performative virtue signaling.

TikTok influencers are famous. Patagonia is immortal.

The influencers built audiences. Patagonia built a movement. The influencers created content. Patagonia created culture. The influencers optimized for likes. Patagonia optimized for legacy.

When Legacy Is Lost

Legacy isn't guaranteed. Just ask Yahoo. Once the homepage of the internet, Yahoo chased acquisitions and short-term ad dollars instead of vision. They went from defining the web to being a punchline, buried under Google's focus and Facebook's dominance.

Or MySpace. They had the world's first real social network empire. But instead of building cultural permanence, they flooded the platform with ads, gimmicks, and noise. The result? Users fled. MySpace didn't die because Facebook was better; it died because MySpace abandoned its own legacy potential.

Chasing trends kills legends. Compromising purpose for quarterly spikes is how immortality rots into irrelevance.

Here's your framework for choosing loyalty over likes:

Metric Shift #1: From Engagement Rate to Retention Rate Stop measuring how many people interact with your content. Start measuring how many people stay with your brand over multiple years.

Metric Shift #2: From Follower Count to Customer Lifetime Value Stop counting audience size. Start calculating revenue per customer over their entire relationship with your brand.

Metric Shift #3: From Viral Moments to Cultural Movements Stop chasing trending topics. Start creating consistent messaging that builds toward long-term cultural change.

Metric Shift #4: From Social Proof to Social Impact Stop collecting testimonials about how great your product is. Start measuring how your brand changes customers' lives, communities, or industries.

The brands that make this shift don't just build businesses; they build institutions that outlast their founders, transcend their industries, and create permanent cultural value.

Stop optimizing for attention that disappears tomorrow. Start building loyalty that compounds forever.

Likes are cheap because they cost nothing to give and create nothing lasting. Loyalty is priceless because it's earned through authentic value and sustained through consistent delivery.

Choose carefully. Your legacy depends on it.

What Do You Want Carved on Your Brand's Tombstone?

Now let me ask you the most important question in brand strategy, the one that will transform how you make every business decision for the rest of your career:

If your brand died tomorrow, what would people say it stood for?

Right now, imagine your brand disappeared tomorrow. What would actually be missing from the world? If the answer is "cheaper products" or "better service," you're building a commodity, not a legacy.

Not what it sold. Not what it claimed to believe. Not what its mission statement declared or its marketing campaigns promoted.

What would people actually say your brand stood for based on their real experience with it?

This is your brand legacy statement; the single sentence that captures the essence of your cultural contribution. It's not your tagline, your value proposition, or your elevator pitch. It's the truth people would tell about the impact your brand had on their lives, their communities, or the world.

Most brands would discover their legacy statement is embarrassingly empty:

"They sold stuff." "They made money." "They existed." "They tried not to offend anyone." "They optimized for shareholder value." "They followed best practices."

Legendary brands have legacy statements that change everything:

Steve Jobs and Apple: "They proved that technology could be beautiful, intuitive, and humanizing rather than just functional."

Walt Disney: "They created a new form of storytelling that brought joy and imagination to generations of families."

Henry Ford: "They democratized transportation and transformed how society organizes itself around mobility."

Coco Chanel: "They liberated women from restrictive fashion and redefined feminine elegance as comfort and confidence."

Each legacy statement describes transformation, not transaction. Impact, not income. Cultural change, not commercial success.

But here's what makes legacy statements powerful: They become decision-making frameworks that guide every choice your company makes.

When Apple faces product development decisions, they ask: "Does this make technology more beautiful, intuitive, and humanizing?" When Disney creates content, they ask: "Does this bring joy and imagination to families?" When Ford considers new initiatives, they ask: "Does this improve how people move through the world?"

The legacy statement becomes the lens through which every business decision gets evaluated.

Steve Jobs didn't just want Apple to be profitable; he wanted to "make a dent in the universe." Jobs didn't just want Apple to be profitable; he wanted every Apple product to make someone more creative, more capable, more human. That obsession drove decisions that often conflicted with short-term optimization but created long-term transformation, turned customers into evangelists, and products into cultural movements.

Jobs killed profitable product lines that didn't serve the legacy vision. He invested in technologies that wouldn't pay off for years. He refused compromises that would have increased quarterly earnings but diminished brand integrity.

The result? Apple didn't just become the most valuable company in the world; it became the most influential technology brand in human history. It changed how we communicate, create, and connect with each other.

That's the power of playing for legacy instead of likes.

Here's your framework for crafting your brand legacy statement:

Step 1: Identify the transformation you create What specific change does your brand bring to customers' lives, industries, or society? Not what you sell, but what transformation happens because you exist.

Step 2: Define your unique approach How do you create this transformation differently from everyone else? What's your distinctive methodology, philosophy, or perspective?

Step 3: Describe the lasting impact What would be different about the world if your brand had never existed?

What would be missing from culture, industry, or human progress?

Step 4: Craft the single sentence Combine transformation, approach, and impact into one clear statement that captures your brand's ultimate purpose.

Step 5: Test every decision against this statement Use your legacy statement as a decision-making filter. Does this choice advance your legacy or distract from it?

Stop reading and do this final assessment: Write your brand's obituary as it would appear today. Then write the obituary you want. The gap between those two is your legacy deficit and your opportunity for immortality.

Worksheet: The Double Obituary

Write two versions of your brand's obituary:

1. **If your brand died today:** What would the headlines say? Would it read like a bland corporate filing "sold products, made money, tried to keep investors happy," or would it actually matter to people's lives?

2. **The obituary you want written in 50 years:** What lasting change, cultural dent, or generational tradition would you want carved into history?

The difference between those two obituaries is your *legacy gap*. That gap is the most important strategy document you'll ever write.

The brands that develop clear, authentic, compelling legacy statements don't just guide their own decisions; they attract customers, employees, and partners who share their vision for transformation.

People don't just buy products from legacy brands; they join movements toward better futures. They don't just work for legacy companies; they contribute to missions that outlast their careers. They don't just recommend legacy brands; they become evangelists for the transformation those brands represent.

Your brand legacy statement is your North Star, the permanent destination that guides all temporary decisions.

Without it, you're optimizing tactics without strategy, pursuing growth without purpose, building revenue without meaning.

With it, every choice becomes an opportunity to advance your lasting contribution to the world.

What do you want carved on your brand's tombstone? That epitaph should guide every decision you make while you're still alive to make them.

How to Build Immortal Brands

Now let me teach you the architecture of immortality: how to build brands so deeply embedded in human culture that they become permanent fixtures of civilization itself.

Immortal brands aren't just businesses; they're cultural institutions that transcend their original purpose and become essential components of how society functions, celebrates, and defines itself.

These aren't accidents of history or results of massive marketing budgets. **Immortal brands are engineered through specific strategic choices that prioritize cultural integration over commercial optimization.**

Let me dissect the most successful immortality project in business history: **The Walt Disney Company's transformation from animation studio to cultural architecture.**

Walt Disney could have built a successful cartoon company. He could have optimized for box office returns, merchandising revenue, and shareholder value. **Instead, he built something that became inseparable from human childhood itself.**

Disney's Immortality Strategy:

And if your board is rolling their eyes at "legacy talk," show them Disney's $74 billion valuation built on a cartoon mouse. Legacy isn't idealistic; it's the most profitable long-term strategy ever invented.

Foundation: Universal Human Experience Disney rooted their brand in storytelling, the most fundamental human activity. Stories aren't trends that fade or technologies that become obsolete; they're permanent features of human nature.

Expansion: Multi-Generational Relevance Disney created content that parents and children could enjoy together, ensuring brand transmission across generations. Each generation didn't just consume Disney; they passed Disney to their children.

Integration: Cultural Ritual Creation Disney movies became family traditions. Disney parks became pilgrimage destinations. Disney characters became shared cultural references that transcended geographic, economic, and social boundaries.

Evolution: Platform Thinking Disney didn't just make cartoons; they created a platform for imagination that could expand into movies, theme parks, merchandise, streaming services, and cultural experiences without losing brand coherence.

Protection: Values Consistency Through decades of leadership changes, market shifts, and cultural evolution,

Disney maintained consistent values around family, imagination, and optimism, keeping the brand identity stable across time.

The result? Disney isn't just a company; it's cultural infrastructure.

Disney didn't just create entertainment; they created the infrastructure of childhood itself. They're not competing with other studios; they're competing with reality for children's imagination.

Disney characters are more recognizable globally than most political leaders. Disney stories shape childhood development across cultures. Disney experiences create family memories that last lifetimes. Disney values influence how entire generations think about optimism, possibility, and the power of imagination.

Disney achieved true immortality: They became necessary to human culture rather than just profitable within it.

Here's your Immortal Brand Framework:

Element #1: Root in Permanent Human Needs Immortal brands address psychological, social, or spiritual needs that don't change with technology or trends. Disney addresses the need for imagination. Apple addresses the need for creative expression. Nike addresses the need for physical achievement.

Element #2: Create Multi-Generational Appeal Immortal brands design experiences that different generations can share, ensuring natural transmission from parents to children. The brand becomes part of family identity rather than individual preference.

Element #3: Build Cultural Rituals Immortal brands create ceremonies, traditions, and shared experiences that become embedded in how society celebrates, mourns, or marks important moments. They become essential components of cultural life.

Element #4: Develop Platform Scalability Immortal brands build around core values and purposes flexible enough to expand into new industries, technologies, and cultural contexts without losing brand coherence.

Element #5: Maintain Values Consistency Immortal brands protect their fundamental principles across leadership changes, market pressures, and cultural shifts. Consistency creates trust that compounds over generations.

Element #6: Embrace Cultural Responsibility Immortal brands understand they're not just businesses; they're cultural institutions with responsibility for positive social impact. They use their influence to improve society rather than just extract value from it.

Here's the immortality test: If your brand disappeared, would an entire generation grow up differently? If not, you're not thinking big enough.

But here's the crucial warning: Immortality requires sacrificing short-term optimization for long-term integration.

Immortal brands often make decisions that hurt quarterly earnings but strengthen cultural position. They invest in projects that won't pay off for decades. They refuse opportunities that would compromise brand integrity for immediate profit.

But don't confuse legacy building with purpose washing. Slapping "we change the world" on your About page isn't legacy creation; it's corporate cosplay. Real legacy brands sacrifice profits for principles, not the other way around.

Most companies aren't willing to make these sacrifices. That's why most companies aren't immortal.

The brands that achieve true immortality understand something that quarterly-focused companies don't: **Cultural permanence is infinitely more valuable than financial performance.**

Cultural permanence creates sustainable competitive advantage that can't be copied or disrupted. It generates customer loyalty that transcends rational decision-making. It attracts talent, partners, and opportunities that pure financial success never could.

Financial performance can be lost in a recession. Cultural permanence survives economic collapse, technological disruption, and competitive pressure.

The immortal brands, Disney, Coca-Cola, Nike, Apple, Mercedes-Benz, aren't just companies that happen to be successful. They're cultural institutions that happen to be profitable.

They didn't just build businesses; they built pieces of civilization that will outlast their founders, their industries, and their original purposes.

Your brand has the same opportunity: To become so essential to human culture that removing it would fundamentally change how society functions.

The question isn't whether you can afford to build for immortality; the question is whether you can afford not to.

Because in the end, only two types of brands survive: Those that become immortal and those that become irrelevant.

Choose immortality. Your legacy depends on it.

Reflection: Profit or Principle?

Legacy demands trade-offs. Use these prompts to pressure-test your decisions:

- Would you kill a profitable product line if it eroded your brand's purpose?
- If investors pressured you to compromise your values, would you walk away from their money?
- Do your decisions optimize for this quarter's revenue, or for your great-grandchildren's reputation?
- If your CEO resigned tomorrow, would your values remain intact, or would they vanish with leadership?

Every legendary brand faced moments where profit and principle collided. Immortals choose principle. The weak choose profit and get forgotten.

The Final Verdict

Here we stand at the end of our beautiful brutality masterclass, where quarterly earnings meet eternal impact, where viral fame confronts lasting legacy, and where you must choose between building a business that dies with its founder or creating an institution that outlasts civilizations.

We started this journey by learning that nice brands die quietly. We end it by understanding that legendary brands live loudly, so loudly they echo across generations.

You now understand the ultimate truth about branding: The only metrics that matter are the ones measured in decades, not days.

Everything else, likes, followers, engagement rates, viral moments, trending topics, is digital exhaust that disappears with the next algorithm update. **Legacy is what remains when all the noise fades away.**

The brands you'll remember on your deathbed aren't the ones with the most followers. They're the ones that changed how you see yourself, how you interact with the world, or how you define what's possible. They're the brands that became part of your identity, your values, your story.

Apple didn't just make computers. They made creativity accessible. Disney didn't just make movies. They made imagination permanent. Nike didn't just make shoes; they made "impossible" obsolete.

Each chose to optimize for transformation over transaction, impact over income, legacy over likes. Each sacrificed short-term validation for long-term cultural integration. Each built something bigger than a business. They built pieces of civilization.

But here's what separates legacy dreamers from legacy builders: the willingness to make decisions that prioritize tomorrow's reputation over today's revenue.

Legacy brands say no to profitable opportunities that compromise their values. They invest in projects that won't pay off for years. They stand for principles even when those principles are expensive, unpopular, or misunderstood.

Most brands aren't willing to make these sacrifices because most brands are run by people playing quarterly games rather than generational games.

They optimize for metrics that reset every month instead of building value that compounds every year. They chase trends instead of creating them. They follow culture instead of shaping it.

The result? They become replaceable participants in someone else's story rather than irreplaceable authors of their own legacy.

Your brand has a choice: **Become digital noise that fades with the next trend, or become a cultural signal that strengthens across generations.**

The noise gets attention. The signal gets immortality. The noise gets likes. The signal gets loyalty. The noise gets fame. The signal gets legend.

But achieving signal over noise requires something most brands lack: the courage to be genuinely themselves in a world that rewards conformity, the patience to build slowly in a culture that demands instant results, and the vision to see beyond quarterly earnings toward generational impact.

This is your final test of beautiful brutality: **Are you brave enough to build something that matters more than it profits? Are you willing to optimize for tombstone inscriptions rather than social media mentions?**

Because when all the metrics fade, when all the campaigns end, when all the trends pass, only one question matters: **What was different about the world because your brand existed?**

That difference, that permanent, irreplaceable cultural contribution, is your brand's legacy. Everything else is just business.

The legendary brands chose legacy. The forgotten brands chose likes.

Time to choose your side of history.

Your legacy is waiting. Your culture is watching. Your immortality is possible.

Your competitors will be footnotes in business school case studies. You could be chapters in human history. Stop building for shareholders and start building for centuries. The choice, and the legacy, is yours.

Your Obituary Drill

Write your brand's obituary as if it died today. Be brutally honest. What would people say?

Now write the obituary you *want* future generations to read. What does the world look like because your brand existed?

The distance between the two is your roadmap. That gap tells you every decision you need to make and every compromise you can no longer afford.

Legacy Playbook: How to Build for Centuries, Not Quarters

Commandment #1: Stop Counting Likes, Start Counting Lifetimes

Engagement metrics vanish the second algorithms shift.

Legacy metrics compound: How many families pass your brand to the next generation? How many people say, "I grew up with this brand, and now my kids will too"?

Test yourself: If your analytics dashboard disappeared tomorrow, would you still know your brand is thriving? If the answer is no, you're worshipping vanity.

Commandment #2: Write Your Obituary Now

Draft the obituary your brand would earn if it died today. Then draft the obituary you *want* written.

That gap? That's your true strategy document.

Repeat this exercise every year. If the gap isn't shrinking, you're drifting toward irrelevance.

Commandment #3: Invest in Cultural Infrastructure, Not Just Campaigns

Campaigns expire. Infrastructure endures.

Disney didn't just run ads; they built parks, rituals, and multi-generational myths.

What permanent structures are you leaving behind? A community platform? A cultural tradition? A universal symbol?

Commandment #4: Trade Short-Term Profits for Long-Term Permanence

Kill profitable products that erode your legacy.

Launch long bets that won't pay off for years but will cement your relevance.

If your board hates it, good. Legacy builders are hated in their own time and worshipped in hindsight.

Commandment #5: Define Your Cultural Dent

Steve Jobs said it best: "Make a dent in the universe."

What's your dent? Democratizing creativity? Redefining health? Liberating fashion?

If your dent isn't obvious in one sentence, your brand is still playing for likes.

Commandment #6: Build Rituals People Pass Down

Think birthdays with Disney movies, Sunday runs with Nike, unboxings with Apple.

Rituals outlast campaigns. Build one tradition tied to your brand and your legacy will spread without you.

Commandment #7: Protect Values Like Sacred Text

Your values aren't marketing slogans. They're holy scripture.

Every new leader, product, or initiative must be filtered through them.

Betray them once for profit, and you've written your own obituary.

Commandment #8: Expand Without Diluting

Legacy brands scale by platform, not by compromise.

Disney went from cartoons to cruises without losing imagination.

Ask: Can this expansion deepen our legacy, or does it dilute it? If it dilutes, kill it fast.

Commandment #9: Take Cultural Responsibility

If you want immortality, you must serve more than yourself.

Patagonia saves the planet. TOMS pioneered buy-one-give-one.

What's your cultural contract? What responsibility do you carry that no one else does?

Commandment #10: Carve Your Legacy Statement in Stone

"The world was different because this brand existed." That's your North Star.

One sentence, permanent, repeatable by your customers, employees, and critics alike.

If you don't have it, you're not building legacy, you're just selling.

Final Directive

Legacy isn't mystical; it's manufactured.

Every product launch, every content drop, every hire, every refusal must be tested against one brutal question:

Does this choice make us more immortal, or more replaceable?

Your competitors are dying for attention. You should be building for remembrance.

Play for centuries. Play for tombstones. Play for history.

CHAPTER 11
The Ethics of Brutality

Brutality Without Boundaries Is Just Abuse

Here's the uncomfortable truth: brutality is a brand's superpower, but like any weapon, it can maim you if you swing it without discipline. Authenticity cuts sharp. Manipulation cuts dirty. And while controversy creates conversation, cruelty creates corpses.

Plenty of brands have forgotten this, and they ended up as cautionary memes instead of legends. Brutality must have a compass. Otherwise, your "bold" stunt becomes a viral obituary.

This chapter is about that compass: the line between being dangerously unforgettable and being unforgettably stupid. We'll talk authenticity versus manipulation, controversy versus cruelty, why Fyre Festival and Theranos burned their names into history's trash heap, and how to use the **Brutality Compass** to keep your shots aimed at the right target.

If you're ready to play with fire, you better learn how not to burn the house down.

Authenticity vs. Manipulation

Brutality without authenticity is fraud with better copywriting.

When you reveal hard truths, fans lean in. When you weaponize lies, fans eventually sharpen knives. That's the brutal difference between authenticity and manipulation.

Take Patagonia: they scream about saving the planet. And guess what? They back it up by donating profits to environmental causes, suing oil companies, and building gear that lasts a decade. Their brutality is authentic, so customers don't just buy jackets; they buy purpose.

Now flip it. Remember Theranos? Elizabeth Holmes sold a dream of painless blood tests with Steve Jobs cosplay and black turtlenecks. The problem? It was bullshit. No science. No truth. Just manipulation dressed up as revolution. Brutality without authenticity didn't just fail; it defrauded patients and nuked an empire.

If your brutality is a costume, eventually someone will rip off the mask.

Controversy vs. Cruelty

Every brand worth remembering picks fights. But not every fight is worth picking.

Here's the rule: controversy attacks systems; cruelty attacks people.

Cards Against Humanity sells offensive humor. Their controversy is calculated, punching at cultural absurdities with sharp wit. They offend with purpose. Customers laugh because they know the game is honest about its own ugliness.

United Airlines, on the other hand, went viral for dragging a paying customer off a plane. That wasn't controversy; that was cruelty. Nobody clapped and said, "Bold move, United." They said, "Holy shit, never again."

Controversy makes people talk. Cruelty makes people walk.

If you're punching down, you're not being bold; you're being a bully.

The Long-Term Damage of Unethical Stunts

Here's where most short-term marketers get it wrong: they confuse shock with strategy.

Shock fades. Scars don't.

Remember Fyre Festival? Marketed as the luxury music event of the decade. Influencers hyped it. Tickets sold out. Then the reality: FEMA tents, cheese sandwiches, and stranded rich kids live-tweeting their misery. Brutality? Yes. Ethical? Hell no. And the fallout? Lawsuits, documentaries, jail time. Fyre isn't a brand; it's a punchline.

Compare that with Ben & Jerry's. They're brutal about politics, taking stances on climate change, refugee rights, and criminal justice. Sure, it pisses some people off. But it's consistent, authentic, and rooted in values they've carried for decades. They win long-term devotion because their brutality has a moral spine.

Ethical brutality compounds. Unethical brutality combusts.

The Brutality Compass

So how do you make sure your next brutal move doesn't turn into a Netflix documentary about failure? Use the **Brutality Compass**.

It has four quadrants:

1. **Honesty:** Is it true? If not, stop.
2. **Style:** Does it make people laugh, nod, or share, or just recoil?
3. **Responsibility:** Does it punch systems, not victims? Does it add to culture rather than subtract from it?

4. **Risk:** Can you live with the fallout? If the backlash went nuclear, would you still stand by it?

Plot every brutal idea on this compass. If it checks all four boxes, launch it with pride. If it fails one, you're flirting with disaster.

Example: Nike's Colin Kaepernick campaign. Honesty? Yes, Kaepernick sacrificed his career. Style? Slick, shareable, iconic. Responsibility? Fighting systemic racism, not targeting individuals. Risk? Huge backlash, but Nike stood tall, and sales spiked.

Now plot Fyre Festival on the same compass. Honesty? Nope. Style? Hype with no substance. Responsibility? Exploitation of customers. Risk? Jail time. That's not brutal branding; that's brand suicide.

The compass doesn't stop you from being dangerous. It stops you from being dead.

A Story of Going Too Far

Years ago, a startup I worked with decided to torch their competition in a campaign. The ad flat-out called rival customers "idiots." Brutal? Yes. Effective? For five minutes. Then came the backlash. Potential partners ghosted. Employees felt ashamed. Customers didn't want to be associated with the nastiness.

The campaign was pulled, not because it wasn't noticed, but because it was too cruel.

If we had used the Brutality Compass, we would've reframed. Attack the system ("outdated, bloated software"), not the people. Make the copy funny instead of hostile. Punch up, not down. The message could have been just as brutal without burning bridges.

The wrong target turns boldness into stupidity.

Brutality is fire. Controlled, it forges steel. Uncontrolled, it burns empires down.

The ethics of brutality boil down to this: **Tell the truth with style, punch systems, not people, take responsibility, and know your risk tolerance.** Do that, and your brand will be feared, loved, and respected. Fail, and you'll be studied in business school under "what not to do."

So next time you're about to launch something outrageous, ask yourself: Does this live on the Brutality Compass, or is this just me playing arsonist with my own reputation?

Because remember: The world doesn't need another Fyre Festival. It needs brands brave enough to be brutal and wise enough to be ethical.

Your Drill: Describe a moment when your brand risked going too far. Now, reframe it with the Brutality Compass.

How could you deliver the same punch without crossing the ethical line?

CHAPTER 12

Global Brutality

Brutal Here, Bland There

Here's the lie most marketers tell themselves: "If it worked in New York, it'll work in Nairobi." Wrong. Brutality doesn't travel with a passport. What feels bold in one culture can feel bland, offensive, or even suicidal in another.

In America, calling your competition "idiots" can be seen as edgy. In Japan, it might be seen as dishonorable. In Germany, your satire better come with substance because empty provocation won't fly. Cultural norms don't erase the need for brutality; they shape it.

This chapter is about taking brutality global. We'll dive into how norms shift the rules, how BrewDog weaponized rebellion in the UK, how Nando's made South Africa laugh at its own politics, how Xiaomi flipped China's market on its head, and why your brutal honesty needs a passport and a translator.

Because remember: there's no such thing as a universal middle finger.

How Culture Shapes Brutality

Brutality works because it breaks expectations. But those expectations change depending on where you plant your flag.

In the U.S., the expectation is polite corporate language, so when you break it, people cheer. In France, cynicism is practically a national sport, so being brutally honest is expected. You'll need to push harder to get attention.

In collectivist cultures (like much of Asia), the line between controversy and disrespect is razor-thin. Mock your competitor too directly, and you look petty. In hyper-individualist cultures, you can roast anyone, and fans will toast you for it.

The universal rule? Brutality isn't about being offensive; it's about being *unexpected*. And "unexpected" depends entirely on cultural context.

Brutality is local. What's savage in San Francisco might be snooze-worthy in Seoul.

Case Study 1: BrewDog (UK)

BrewDog built a beer empire on two words: *Punk IPA.*

They didn't just sell beer; they declared war on the entire brewing industry. Their ads trashed corporate giants, mocked the stuffy traditions of British pubs, and even launched stunts like "Equity for Punks," letting fans literally buy into the rebellion. They once drove a tank down Camden High Street to protest bland beer. Subtle? Hell no. Effective? Absolutely.

In the UK, where polite understatement is the default, BrewDog's loud, brash irreverence felt like a cultural middle finger. Their brutality resonated because it punched up at the establishment, and the Brits, with their love of irony, couldn't resist.

But here's the twist: when BrewDog expanded to the U.S., their shock tactics didn't hit as hard. Why? Because Americans already had a hundred microbreweries screaming rebellion. Brutality has to evolve with the market.

Your rebellion only works if people recognize the empire you're rebelling against.

Case Study 2: Nando's (South Africa)

If you want a masterclass in culturally tuned brutality, look at Nando's ads in South Africa.

They don't just sell peri-peri chicken; they roast the country's politics with it. During election seasons, Nando's drops satirical ads mocking corrupt politicians, dodgy promises, and the circus of democracy. They've lampooned everything from xenophobia to presidential scandals.

Here's the genius: South Africa is a place where political tension is constant, and humor is survival. Nando's found a way to let people laugh at chaos while making themselves unforgettable.

But imagine dropping the same ads in, say, Singapore or Saudi Arabia. That kind of political parody could get you banned. Or worse. Brutality only works when the culture allows space for satire.

Nando's proves you can weaponize laughter, but only if the crowd is ready to laugh.

Case Study 3: Xiaomi (China)

In the early 2010s, China's smartphone market was a battlefield dominated by giants like Apple and Samsung. Xiaomi didn't try to out-luxury Apple. They didn't try to out-global Samsung. Instead, they got brutally honest about what people actually wanted: sleek phones at half the price, built with feedback from the community.

They called themselves "the people's brand." They turned product launches into mass events where fans felt like insiders, not customers. They weren't afraid to admit flaws or push updates based on user complaints. That level of transparency was radical in a culture where big companies usually hide behind red tape.

The brutality? Positioning themselves as the anti-Apple: less status symbol, more straight shooter. And it worked. Xiaomi became a juggernaut precisely because they embraced honesty where competitors clung to polish.

Sometimes the most brutal move isn't provocation; it's saying what everyone already knows but no brand dares admit.

Adapting Brutal Honesty to Cultural Markets

So how do you take your brutal brand global without turning into the next Pepsi protest ad?

1. **Learn the local taboos.** What's edgy in one culture is offensive in another. Brutality doesn't mean disrespecting the sacred.
2. **Punch the right villain.** Who's the enemy? In the U.S., it might be corporate greed. In Brazil, it might be bureaucracy. In Japan, inefficiency. If you're not fighting the right villain, your brutality won't resonate.
3. **Translate tone, not just language.** A sarcastic tweet that kills in English may flop in Mandarin. Find the cultural equivalent of your voice, not just the dictionary translation.
4. **Test, then escalate.** Drop small brutal truths and see how the market reacts before you set off fireworks.

Brutality is universal, but the script has to be local.

The Global Brutality Heat Map

Not every culture has the same appetite for brutal honesty. Some markets cheer when you torch a competitor. Others clutch their pearls. The **Global Brutality Heat Map** helps you gauge how far you can push before crossing into cultural suicide.

Quadrants

1. High Tolerance, High Response (The Wild West)

Examples: U.S., UK, Brazil

Audiences reward boldness. Roast competitors, provoke controversy, and satire lands hard.

Danger: noise saturation. Everyone's screaming, so you need both brutality *and* brilliance to stand out.

Here, polite brands die first.

2. High Tolerance, Low Response (The Iron Curtain)

Examples: France, Germany, Australia

People respect bluntness, but they don't throw parades for it. Brutality must come with depth; substance matters as much as swagger.

Danger: empty provocation. If your "truth" is shallow, you look like a clown, not a crusader.

Brutality without brains is just noise pollution.

3. Low Tolerance, High Response (The Tightrope)

Examples: Japan, South Korea, Singapore

A single misstep can get you exiled. Brutality must be precise, clever, and aimed at acceptable villains (waste, inefficiency, hypocrisy).

Danger: punching the wrong target can get you blacklisted fast.

One sharp arrow beats a hundred loud cannons.

4. Low Tolerance, Low Response (The Ice Zone)

Examples: Saudi Arabia, conservative Middle East, parts of Africa

Brutality often clashes with cultural, religious, or political taboos. Playing too bold risks bans, or worse.

Danger: arrogance. Assuming your Western playbook will work here is a fast track to irrelevance.

Subtle rebellion beats headline-grabbing explosions.

How to Use the Heat Map

1. Place your target market on the map.
2. Match your brutality strategy to the tolerance/response level.

3. Adjust voice, villains, and velocity accordingly.

Remember: Brutality is universal, but its expression must be tuned like an instrument. Too soft and no one hears you. Too loud and you're banned from the concert.

Brutality without borders is a fantasy. The truth is simpler: every market has its own sacred cows, its own villains, its own appetite for confrontation. Your job is to find them, slaughter them, and serve them medium rare, with just the right cultural seasoning.

Remember this: Brutal honesty travels, but only if you pack the right passport.

So here's your drill:

Pick one country outside your home market. Map your brutal strategy there. How would it land? What would need to change? Where's the line between bold and banned?

Because the future isn't American, or British, or Chinese. It's global. And if you want your brand to matter worldwide, your brutality better know how to cross borders.

The middle finger looks different in every culture. Learn the gesture, or get left waving at yourself.

CHAPTER 13

From Brutality to Rebirth

Beige Is Death. Brutality Is Resurrection

Let's start with a funeral. Picture your brand lying in a beige coffin: polite messaging, safe campaigns, stock-photo smiles. The audience yawns, checks their phones, and leaves before the eulogy ends.

That's what happens when a brand goes soft. It doesn't explode; it decays. And no amount of marketing perfume can cover the stench of beige.

But here's the beautiful, brutal truth: death is not the end. Beige brands can come back from the grave. They can be resurrected, not with niceness, but with the electric jolt of brutal relevance.

This chapter is about rebirth, the process of dragging your brand out of the morgue and into the arena, bloodied but alive. We'll walk through the Rebirth Framework (Audit → Kill Beige → Name Villain → Build Ritual → Crown Heroes) and learn from brands like Crocs, Lego, and Old

Spice, which were once left for dead but came back swinging.

If your brand's already in rigor mortis, good news: resurrection starts now.

The Rebirth Framework

Your brand just died of beige. Now here's how to drag it back from the grave. Follow the five stages, step by step.

Step 1: Audit (The Autopsy)

Every resurrection starts with an autopsy. Brutally audit your brand. What's working? What's dead? What reeks of beige? Write it down, no excuses. If you can't face the corpse, you can't revive it.

Ask: *What killed us?*

- Which products, campaigns, or messages fell flat?
- Where did we stop being bold?
- Which parts of the brand still have a pulse?

Make two lists: "Alive" and "Dead." Keep only what makes hearts race.

Step 2: Kill Beige (The Execution)

Beige is polite mediocrity. It's the brand equivalent of hospital food: it feeds no one, excites no one, and makes no one remember you. Killing beige means cutting safe taglines, vanilla campaigns, and the kind of logos that look like they were spit out by a bored intern in Canva.

Ask: *What must die to make room for the living?*

- Safe taglines
- Polite mission statements
- Campaigns designed to "offend no one"
- Logos and visuals that could belong to anyone

Cross out every beige element. Kill it with ink before you kill it in public.

Step 3: Name Villain (The Enemy)

Every rebirth needs an enemy. Who killed you in the first place? Complacency? Boring competitors? A broken system? Name your villain out loud. Resurrections demand revenge.

Ask: *Who or what do we fight now?*

- A lazy competitor?
- A broken system?
- A cultural lie?

Write this sentence: *"Our brand exists to destroy _____."*

Step 4: Build Ritual (The Resurrection)

Give your fans a reason to gather, celebrate, and signal their belonging. Rituals are the holy water of brand rebirth.

Without them, you're just another zombie stumbling around, pretending to live.

Ask: *How do we make fans feel alive again?*

- What action can we formalize into a ritual?
- What language or symbol unites the tribe?
- How do we celebrate their milestones?

Pick one habit customers already do. Turn it into a ceremony.

Step 5: Crown Heroes (The Coronation)

Every resurrection needs disciples. Find the customers who stuck around during your beige years, elevate them as heroes, and let them carry the banner of your rebirth. Nothing proves you're alive again like an army of fanatics marching in your name.

Ask: *Who leads the charge?*

- Loyal fans who stuck with you through beige years
- Employees who bleed for the mission
- Customers who evangelize hardest

Elevate them publicly. Give them status. Let them be your resurrection proof.

Resurrection isn't magic. It's murder (of beige), vengeance (naming villains), and rebirth (through ritual and heroes).

Case Study: Crocs. From Punchline to Powerhouse

For years, Crocs were the world's ugliest shoe. They were mocked on late-night TV, sneered at by fashion critics, and relegated to gardeners and nurses. If shoes had an obituary, Crocs' would've read: *"Died of ugliness. Survived by ridicule."*

But then Crocs leaned into the ugliness. Instead of running from the insult, they weaponized it. They launched bold collaborations with Balenciaga, dropped neon colors, and turned their meme status into fuel. They went from *"LOL, hideous"* to *"ironically cool"* to *"cultural juggernaut."*

Crocs' resurrection was brutal honesty: *Yes, we're ugly. That's the point.*

Case Study: Lego. Back from the Brink

In the early 2000s, Lego was suffocating. Sales tanked, competitors copied their products, and kids were ditching blocks for video games. Lego was one bad quarter away from being a fond memory.

So what did they do? They killed beige. They stopped chasing random product lines and refocused on their core brutal truth: creativity through play. Then they named their villain: passive entertainment. Instead of trying to out-

Mattel Mattel, Lego positioned itself as the antidote to screen addiction.

The result? Global rebirth. Lego movies, theme parks, cultural relevance. Today, Lego isn't just a toy company; it's a creative empire.

Case Study: Old Spice. Dead Man Walking to Viral Legend

Once upon a time, Old Spice was your grandpa's deodorant. The brand was a walking ghost: outdated, irrelevant, beige.

Then came "The Man Your Man Could Smell Like." Brutal, funny, self-aware. They mocked their own irrelevance, roasted competitors, and turned a forgotten aisle product into a cultural icon.

The ad didn't just go viral; it resurrected an entire category. Old Spice proved that self-deprecating brutality is often the sharpest weapon of all.

Sometimes the best resurrection strategy is to laugh at your own corpse.

The Resurrection Drill

Imagine your brand has just died of beige. Write its resurrection story.

1. **The Obituary:** How did it die? Was it boredom, irrelevance, cowardice?
2. **The Villain:** Who gets the blame? Safe leadership? Trend-chasing mediocrity? A system that smothered originality?
3. **The Ritual:** What new customer habit or celebration can bring it back?
4. **The Hero:** Who leads the charge: your fans, your employees, or your boldest product?
5. **The Resurrection Statement:** Write the brutal truth that brings it roaring back.

Example:

"Brand X died quietly, ignored into irrelevance. It rose again when it admitted the truth: nobody cared because it had nothing worth saying. Now it fights against empty corporate promises, crowns its customers as rebels, and celebrates every purchase like a war cry. The beige brand is dead. Long live the brutal brand."

Rebirth isn't about spin. It's about slaughter. You kill beige, you crown heroes, and you turn scars into sermons. Crocs did it by owning their ugliness. Lego did it by defending imagination. Old Spice did it by laughing at its own ghost.

Your brand can too, but only if you're willing to admit the death certificate is real, and the only cure is brutal resurrection.

So here's your takeaway: If your brand is beige, bury it. Then dig it up, slap it awake, and drag it back to life screaming.

Because in branding, resurrection isn't optional. It's survival of the most brutal.

The Choice Is Yours

The funeral for nice brands starts tomorrow. Will you be in the coffin or giving the eulogy?

By now, you've seen the evidence. You know the neuroscience behind why outrage hijacks attention. You understand why polarization creates loyalty and safety breeds invisibility. You've witnessed brands that chose beautiful brutality and built empires, and brands that chose comfort and died quietly.

The comfortable lies have been exposed. The vanilla strategies have been demolished. The weapons have been loaded and aimed.

Now comes the hard part: choosing.

The Two Paths Forward

You stand at a fork in the road. Down one path lies everything you've been taught about branding: the focus groups, the inoffensive messaging, the desperate attempt to make everyone happy. It's a well-worn trail, traveled by millions of forgettable brands before you.

Down the other path lies beautiful brutality. The courage to offend some people in service of obsessing others. The backbone to stand for something worth defending. The clarity to choose your enemies as carefully as you choose your allies.

One path leads to polite applause and quiet death. The other leads to passionate devotion and living forever in the minds that matter.

The choice has always been yours. The only difference now is that you can no longer pretend you don't know the consequences.

Your Brand's Obituary

Here's a thought experiment that should terrify every marketer: write your brand's obituary as it stands today.

"[Your Brand Name], founded in [year], died quietly after years of trying not to offend anyone. Despite having quality products and good intentions, they will be remembered for nothing in particular. They are survived by countless other brands that made the same choice to play it safe until they played themselves into irrelevance."

Does that sting? Good. Pain means you're still alive enough to feel something.

Now rewrite it:

"[Your Brand Name] died as they lived: unapologetically. They chose enemies and earned devotion. They stood for something and fell for nothing. They will be missed by those who loved them and remembered by those who hated them. In the end, they mattered."

Which obituary do you want? Because you're writing it with every choice you make.

The Brutality Pledge

If you're ready to stop dying quietly, make this pledge:

I will no longer apologize for having opinions.
I will choose my enemies as carefully as I choose my allies.
I will polarize with purpose rather than please without passion.
I will be brutally honest rather than safely irrelevant.
I will build something worth hating. And worth loving even more.

This isn't a marketing strategy. It's a manifesto for brands that refuse to die quietly.

The Last Word

The attention economy is a zero-sum game. Every moment someone spends thinking about your competitor is a moment they're not thinking about you. Every emotion they feel for another brand is emotion unavailable to yours.

Nice brands accept this scarcity and try to take what's left. Brutal brands reject it and demand what they deserve.

The revolution starts with a simple recognition: your brand is already a weapon. The only questions are whether you have the courage to aim it and the conviction to pull the trigger.

Stop asking permission to matter. Stop apologizing for having something to say. Stop trying to be everyone's second choice when you could be someone's only choice.

The graveyard of business is full of brands that played it safe. The hall of fame belongs to the ones that played for keeps.

Your obituary is being written every day. What story will it tell?

The choice is yours. Choose brutality. Choose memory. Choose to matter.

Now go build something magnificent and piss off all the right people doing it.

About the Author

Terry Shand builds brands that don't ask for attention, they hijack it. An English-born entrepreneur and marketing and sales insurgent, he's spent the last decade helping founders torch beige strategies, weaponize their stories, and dominate the modern attention war.

From AI platforms to high-ticket education empires, Terry has launched ventures, trained thousands, and engineered branding strategies that turn polite businesses into cultural wrecking balls. His work fuses brutal honesty with seductive storytelling, the exact formula he uses to build movements, not just marketing campaigns.

Beautiful Brutality is his battle manual for anyone ready to stop whispering in hurricanes and start making people pick a side.